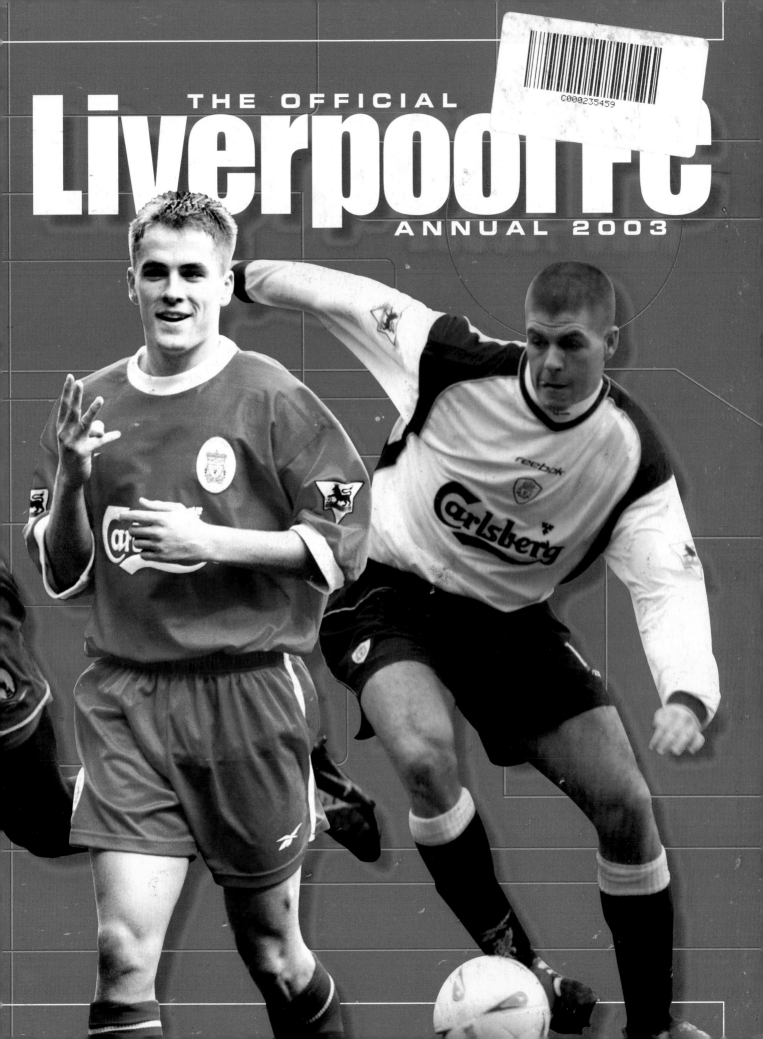

THE OFFICIAL
Liverpool FC
ANNUAL 2003

C000235459

LIVERPOOL FC

THE OFFICIAL LIVERPOOL FC ANNUAL 2003

CONTENTS

YOU'LL NEVER WALK ALONE

LIVERPOOL FOOTBALL CLUB

EST·1892

30

DOUBLE OVER MAN U

THOMMO

AFTER GÉRARD HOULLIER'S SUDDEN AND TERRIFYING ILLNESS IN OCTOBER 2001, LIVERPOOL FANS HELD THEIR BREATH. WAS THE SEASON OVER? COULD ANYONE FILL HOULLIER'S BOOTS – EVEN TEMPORARILY? PHIL THOMPSON SOON ANSWERED THOSE QUESTIONS, AND AS THE GAMES WENT BY AND THE TEAM WENT FROM STRENGTH TO STRENGTH EVERYONE RELAXED. BUT HOW DID THOMMO FEEL?

loved every minute. It was a challenge," he admits.

"There was no warning that it was coming. Gérard was taken ill very quickly and it was a case of doing my best for as long as was necessary. I would do anything for this club, I care about it passionately, and I just wanted to keep things ticking over as best I could.

"The club was excellent in that they said right from the start they would not be bringing in an outsider to help. They had trust and faith in us and that's exactly what Gérard would have wanted.

"We had a good start after I took over and we went on a long winning run. That was very important because it gave everyone confidence about what we were trying to do. Gérard was always in our thoughts and at the end of every team talk we said his name to the players. We told them to go out there and win for the boss.

"It was particularly difficult in the early stages because we weren't sure how bad the illness was. The day after his operation we flew to Kiev for a Champions League game and that was a very hard trip. We didn't really know what was going on but we told the players as much as we could. It was a great achievement to win that match in the Ukraine and it was the perfect pick-me-up for everyone."

While Gérard Houllier has publicly admitted he was pleased to be kept in touch with developments as soon as he came out of intensive care, Thompson was also more than happy to call the boss for advice – often several times a day.

"I don't think people realise how much we kept in touch. We were on the phone quite a lot, let's put it that way. He is a great manager and it was important that we kept him in touch with what was happening.

"We didn't over-burden him at the start because that wouldn't have been right, but as he got stronger we started to drip-feed him with more information and it's probably right that his recovery was aided by being involved. That's how much he loves the game."

Thompson doesn't hesitate when asked what the hardest and most surprising aspect of his new job was. "The media, without a doubt," he said.

"I just couldn't believe how much media work was involved in the job. It was relentless. It was almost every day at times, especially when we had midweek games. It takes up a lot of time but it's an important part of the job. I like to think that I got by and that maybe some people in the media now see me in a slightly different light."

There's little doubt that football fans all over the country now see Thommo in a different light. Not only a good assistant manager, but also more than capable of looking after the team affairs of the most successful club in English football.

True, football is a team game and the backroom team at Anfield is second to none, but Thommo was in charge for five months and deserves all the plaudits which come his way.

"I'm proud of what we did during that time. My aim was to keep the season going and I think we achieved that. When Gérard returned for that amazing night against Rome we were challenging for the title and on the verge of qualifying for the Champions League quarter finals.

"The biggest challenge for me was to keep the club in Europe because I know how much Gérard loves his European football.

"There were down times around Christmas when results slipped away from us but I was always confident we would come through it. The attitude of these players is first class and it was always going to be just a matter of time before we turned things around again. Every club has a bad spell at some stage, but we did come good again and the lads deserve a lot of respect for that.

"In fact the way the players coped with the whole situation was incredible. They lost their manager for five months of the season but still found the inner strength to keep performing to exceptionally high levels.

"Everyone should be proud of the effort they gave. They are all an absolute credit to Liverpool Football Club." ●

"I would do anything for this club, I care about it passionately…"

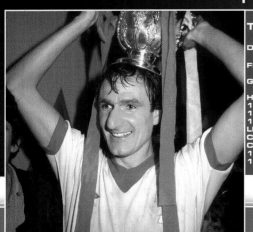

THOMMO'S LIVERPOOL CAREER

DEBUT: 28 OCTOBER 1972 V NORWICH CITY

FIRST TEAM APPEARANCES: 477

GOALS: 13

HONOURS:
1ST DIVISION CHAMPIONSHIP 1972/73, 1975/76, 1976/77, 1978/79, 1979/80, 1981/82 & 1982/83; FA CUP 1974; LEAGUE/MILK CUP 1981 & 1982; EUROPEAN CUP 1978 & 1981; UEFA CUP 1973 & 1976; CHARITY SHIELD 1974, 1976, 1977 (SHARED), 1979, 1980 & 1982; EUROPEAN SUPER CUP 1977

12th August 2001: Liverpool begin their season as they finished the last – winning silverware. The Reds returned to Cardiff – the scene of their double domestic cup triumph the previous season – to record a morale boosting 2–1 victory over Manchester United in the Charity Shield. Michael Owen netted both goals in the first half while Ruud van Nistelrooy pulled back a consolation strike after the break.

18th August 2001: Michael Owen got Liverpool's Premiership season off to a winning start with both goals in the 2–1 victory over West Ham. Paolo Di Canio had levelled the scores from the penalty spot, but Owen proved to be the opening day hero with a priceless double at Anfield.

Westerveld would later join Real Sociedad in Spain.

6th September 2001: Jerzy Dudek and Chris Kirkland both arrived on the same day in a dramatic double swoop. Dudek was signed from Feyenoord and was immediately confirmed as Liverpool's number one goalkeeper while Kirkland, an England under-21 international, cost the best part of £7 million and was described as "Liverpool's goalkeeper for the future" by Houllier.

11th September 2001: Liverpool entered the Champions League competition for the first time when they took on Portuguese side Boavista at Anfield. The Reds had to settle for a 1–1 draw after coming back from a goal down early in the game.

Houllier. "It was only much later that I discovered I had only a 20 per cent chance of survival."

30th October 2001: Liverpool qualified for the second phase of the Champions League with a well earned 2–0 victory over Borussia Dortmund in their final group game at Anfield. A goal in each half from Vladimir Smicer and Stephen Wright was enough to see the Reds into round two of the competition.

2001/02
SEASON REVIEW

THE STUNNING SUCCESS OF THE 2000–01 TREBLE-WINNING SEASON WAS ALWAYS GOING TO BE A HARD ACT TO FOLLOW. CHARITY SHIELD AND SUPER CUP VICTORIES, A BEST-EVER SECOND-PLACE FINISH IN THE PREMIERSHIP AND A QUARTER-FINAL BERTH IN THE CHAMPIONS LEAGUE WERE JUST A FEW OF THE HIGHLIGHTS IN AN EVENTFUL CAMPAIGN. HERE ARE THE 20 DEFINING MOMENTS OF LIVERPOOL'S 2001–02 SEASON.

24th August 2001: Gérard Houllier's side got one over on the Germans with a 3–1 victory against Bayern Munich in Monaco to win the European Super Cup. Emile Heskey, John Arne Riise and Michael Owen were all on the scoresheet as the Reds collected their fifth trophy of 2001.

6th September 2001: Gérard Houllier admitted it was a case of his head ruling his heart when he made the decision to replace Sander Westerveld as Liverpool's goalkeeper. "Sometimes you don't like making decisions, but they must be made," said Houllier. "I felt I could improve the team and that's what I did."

9th October 2001: Liverpool's defence of the Worthington Cup is ended in the early stages as Grimsby secure a shock victory at Anfield. Former Everton midfielder Phil Jevons is the First Division side's hero, with a stunning goal in the closing stages of extra time. "My players gave everything, but tonight just wasn't our night," said Gérard Houllier.

13th October 2001: Gérard Houllier was dramatically taken to hospital at half time of Liverpool's 1–1 draw with Leeds United. The Reds boss complained of chest pains and later underwent life-saving heart surgery which was to keep him out of action for five months. "At the time I didn't know how serious it was," said

29th November 2002: Robbie Fowler brought his long love affair with Liverpool to an end when he signed for Leeds United for a fee in excess of £12 million. "Robbie asked to leave because he didn't like the rotation system at the club and didn't want to sign a new contract," said assistant boss Phil Thompson at the time. Fowler added: "I had a great time at Liverpool but sometimes you need a change and I feel this is the right move to make at the right time in my career."

22nd December 2001: Liverpool acted quickly to replace the void left by Fowler when they snapped up former Arsenal striker

2001-2002 ■ 2001-2002 ■ 2001-2002 ■ 2001-2002 ■ 2001-2002 ■

Nicolas Anelka on loan until the end of the season. The French international would go on to score five goals in 15 appearances for the Reds.

23rd December 2001: Liverpool went down to a disappointing 2–1 home defeat at the hands of Arsenal, despite seeing the Gunners reduced to ten men when midfielder Giovanni van Bronckhorst was sent off in the first half. Thierry Henry scored on the stroke of half time from the penalty spot and Arsenal's lead was doubled after the break by Freddie Ljungberg. Jari Litmanen pulled one back to set up a grandstand finish, but the Gunners held on to record a crucial victory.

27th January 2002: Gérard Houllier's hopes of defending the FA Cup are ended at Highbury as Denis Bergkamp's goal sends Liverpool crashing out of the competition. There was further trouble for the Reds when Jamie Carragher was sent off for throwing a coin back into the crowd after it had been aimed at him by an Arsenal supporter.

3rd February 2002: Liverpool thrash one of their expected championship rivals with a four-goal blitz at Leeds. In a game which saw Robbie Fowler make his first appearance against the Reds since leaving Anfield, goals from Ferdinand (og), Heskey (2) and Owen leave the home crowd spellbound. Without a doubt, this was one of Liverpool's best performances of the campaign.

9th February 2002: If the performance at Leeds was exceptional, then the one at Ipswich the following weekend was probably even better. Liverpool produced a superb brand of flowing football to rattle up their highest score of the season in a 6–0 rout. The goals were scored by Abel Xavier, on his debut, Heskey (2), Owen (2) and captain Hyypia.

19th March 2002: Gérard Houllier makes an emotional return after five months out of action as Liverpool survive the so-called group of death to reach the last eight of the Champions League. Knowing a 2–0 win would be good enough to see them through, the Reds did the business as Jari Litmanen and Emile Heskey sent

an ecstatic Anfield crowd home singing loud and proud into the night.

30th March 2002: Liverpool's title dreams are kept alive as Vladimir Smicer smashes the ball into the back of the net with virtually the last kick of the game to give the Reds a 1–0 victory over Chelsea. A draw would have seen Liverpool slip further behind leaders Arsenal, but the Czech midfielder's last-gasp goal kept their dreams of Premiership glory on track.

9th April 2002: Liverpool's hopes of Champions League glory were finally ended on a night of drama in Leverkusen. Leading 1–0 from the first leg at Anfield, the Reds were favourites to reach the last four of the competition, especially when Xavier equalised Ballack's opener for the home side on the stroke of half time. And when Litmanen scored a crucial goal with just 12 minutes to play, Liverpool were back in the box-seat after conceding two daft goals early in the second half. But Lucio bagged another for the home side who moved into the semi-finals by a 4–3 aggregate after a 4–2 victory on the night.

11th May 2002: Liverpool round off their season with a thumping 5–0 victory over Ipswich to secure second place in the Premiership table. The result confirmed Ipswich's relegation to the First Division and ensured Liverpool enjoyed their highest finish since the start of the Premier League. Goals were rattled home by Riise (2), Smicer, Owen and Anelka.

21st May 2002: Gérard Houllier decides not to press ahead with the permanent signing of Nicolas Anelka. After spending a week mulling over the decision – with the transfer fee and personal terms already having been agreed – the Reds boss decides to look elsewhere for the player needed to replace Robbie Fowler in the Anfield strike force.

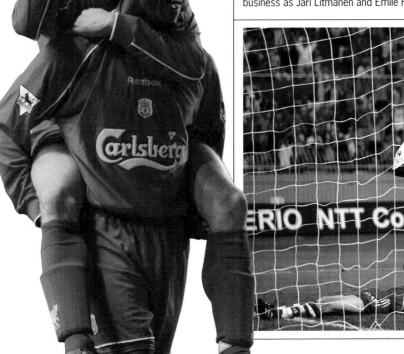

15 FACTS ABOUT...

STEPHANE HENCHOZ

1 Stephane was born in Billens, Switzerland on 7th September 1974.

2 He is a Swiss international.

3 Stephane was signed from Blackburn Rovers for £3.5 million in the summer of 1999.

4 His debut for Liverpool came against Hull City in a Worthington Cup tie at Anfield in September 1999.

5 His squad number for Liverpool is 2.

6 Stephane played in the 1994 World Cup Finals for Switzerland.

7 Despite the fact Blackburn were relegated in 1999, Henchoz was voted player of the year.

8 He played for Switzerland in Euro 96 in England.

9 Stephane's first club was his local team Stade Payerne.

10 Besides playing for Roy Hodgson when he was manager of Switzerland, Henchoz has played club football for Hodgson at Neuchatel Xamax and Blackburn Rovers.

11 Stephane has also played in Germany for SV Hamburg.

12 In Liverpool's treble season 2000/01 Stephane played 53 games without scoring.

13 Stephane made his international debut for Switzerland as a 20-year-old.

14 Stephane played his first senior game against Real Madrid at the Bernabeu Stadium for Swiss side FC Bulle.

15 Stephane has formed a fearsome central defensive pairing with Sami Hyypia and in their first season at Anfield led Liverpool to the best defensive record in the league.

1 — Abel Xavier was born on 30th November 1972.

2 — He took over the number 3 shirt when he arrived at Anfield, previously worn by Christian Ziege.

3 — He was a member of Portugal's 2002 World Cup squad.

4 — He signed for Liverpool on 31st January for an undisclosed fee.

5 — He became the third player to leave Everton for Liverpool, following in the footsteps of Dave Hickson and Nick Barmby.

6 — He has previously played for European giants Benfica and PSV Eindhoven.

7 — He began his playing career with little known side Estrela Amadora.

8 — He first unveiled his eccentric hairstyle while playing for Portugal in Euro 2000.

9 — During Euro 2000, Abel was sent off for a foul on Zinedine Zidane in the last minute of a crunch game. His vehement protestations led to him being handed a nine-month ban from international football.

15 FACTS ABOUT...

ABEL XAVIER

10 — He scored on his Liverpool debut in the 6–0 demolition of Ipswich at Portman Road.

11 — He is comfortable operating anywhere across the defensive line.

12 — Xavier was close to agreeing new terms with Everton before Liverpool swooped for his signature.

13 — In total he made 49 appearances for Liverpool's city rivals – without scoring a goal. He already has two to his name at Liverpool.

14 — Abel was born in Mozambique but qualifies for Portuguese nationality.

15 — He drives a classic "Smart car".

15 FACTS ABOUT...
SAMI HYYPIA

1 He was born in Porvoo, Finland on 7th October 1973.

2 His first squad number for Liverpool was 12.

3 His current squad number is 4.

4 His present contract expires in 2005.

5 Sami was Gérard Houllier's fifth signing as Liverpool manager when he arrived from Dutch club Willem II for £2.6 million in May 1999.

6 Sami made his Liverpool debut at Hillsborough in a 2–1 win over Sheffield Wednesday in August 1999.

7 His first goal for Liverpool came in a 3–2 defeat by Manchester United at Anfield.

8 Sami spent seven days on trial at Newcastle in 1996 but was rejected by manager Kevin Keegan. A philosophical Hyypia said at the time: "It's not a problem, people sometimes make mistakes!"

9 Sami is a Finland international and a regular in his country's side.

10 Sami became a Liverpool fan in 1984 after watching the Reds beat Roma to win the European Cup. His hero at the time was a certain Ian Rush.

11 Sami was watched three times by Reds Chief Scout Ron Yeats before Liverpool signed him.

12 Sami is vice captain of Liverpool and jointly lifted the FA Cup and Super Cup with Jamie Redknapp and Robbie Fowler, he lifted the UEFA Cup together with Robbie Fowler and then the Charity Shield on his own as captain.

13 In the treble season Sami scored four goals in 58 appearances.

14 Sami made his 100th appearance for Liverpool against Charlton at the Valley when Gérard Houllier's team achieved Champions League qualification on the final day of last season.

15 He made his 150th appearance in March as Liverpool beat Charlton 2–0 at Anfield.

1 Milan was born in Ostrava, Czech Republic, on 28th October 1981.

2 He wears squad number five for Liverpool.

3 He joined Liverpool for £3.5 million from Banik Ostrava in December 2001.

4 He is a full international for the Czech Republic.

5 Milan made his Liverpool debut against Barcelona in the Champions League at the Nou Camp on 13th March 2002.

6 Before he arrived at Anfield Milan was widely regarded as one of the hottest properties in Europe.

7 He first came to Gérard Houllier's attention playing for the Czech under-21 team at the European under-21 championships in 2000.

8 He scored nine goals in 14 games for the Czech under-21 team.

9 Baros represented the Czech Olympic team at the Sydney Olympics, in the summer of 2000.

10 Besides Liverpool, Borussia Dortmund, Juventus and Inter Milan were keen on signing him.

11 He made his international debut for the Czech Republic national team against Belgium in 2000.

12 He scored his first international goal for his country on his second cap against Northern Ireland.

13 At Banik Ostrava he was dubbed the Ostravan Maradona because of his silky skills.

14 He scored his first goal for Liverpool in his third reserve game at Bradford City.

15 He signed for Liverpool in the summer of 2001 but had to wait until he was granted a work permit before arriving at Anfield in December, on the same day Nicolas Anelka was signed.

15 FACTS ABOUT...

MILAN BAROS

EMILE HESKEY

I know it's an old cliché but it's true to say that my dreams came true when I signed for Liverpool. Don't get me wrong, it was a wrench to leave Leicester because they were good for me as a club and I was given my big chance there, but you just can't turn down a move to a club the size of Liverpool. They were my team as a boy. Now that I'm here, I want to stay, where is there to go from here? Any move would be a step down and I know I can realise all of my footballing dreams here.

JARI LITMANEN

Growing up in Finland I used to watch lots of Liverpool games on the television. They were the dominant side in European football in the late seventies and early eighties and the likes of Dalglish and Keegan were brilliant to watch. They were my heroes and players I wanted to copy whenever I was on the field. I studied Liverpool's history and wanted to know as much about the club as I could. Now I want to help them become the dominant side in European football once again.

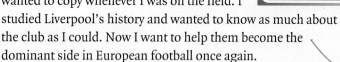

EVER SINCE LIVERPOOL FOOTBALL CLUB SPLIT FROM EVERTON WAY BACK IN THE 1890S, LIVERPOOL HAS BEEN A CITY DIVIDED INTO TWO COLOURS: THE REDS AND THE BLUES. MUCH TO OUR DELIGHT, WE'VE FOUND SOME INCREDIBLE TALENT AMONGST THE LIFE-LONG REDS FANS. BUT, WE'VE ALSO MANAGED TO CONVERT A FEW OF THE BLUES MOST TALENTED FANS ALONG THE WAY.

THE REDS

CHRIS KIRKLAND

Liverpool were my team from an early age. I always watched as many games as I could on television and, whenever possible, I would travel up to Anfield to

watch from the Kop. My Dad and I used to get the bus from Hinckley up to Liverpool and it was always a great day out. Of course, standing in the Kop I always dreamed of one day playing out there on the field but I don't suppose I ever expected that dream to come true. Needless to say, when the chance came up for me to sign for Liverpool I didn't need to be asked twice. It was one of the proudest days of my life when I signed my contract here.

STEVEN GERRARD

I've been a Liverpool fan all my life. I know a lot is made of the fact that so many of the young lads to come through the ranks here supported Everton as a boy, but I have always been red through and through. The likes of Ronnie Whelan and John Barnes were my idols and to have the chance of following in their footsteps is brilliant. Coming through the Academy, I always hoped I would keep improving and be good enough to make the first team one day. Thankfully that has happened for me. I know how lucky I am because I know what it's like to be a young kid wanting to play for your favourite club.

MICHAEL OWEN

My Dad used to play for Everton so naturally they were the team I followed as a kid. But as soon as I was taken on by Liverpool and started playing for the youth side here that changed very quickly and for a long time now I have been one hundred per cent Liverpool. I definitely don't have any split loyalties. Liverpool are my team and Liverpool are the club I want to do well and score lots of goals for.

STEPHEN WRIGHT

I was an Everton fan as a kid and I had the chance to be taken on there when I was younger. But I felt that Liverpool's training facilities and coaching staff were better so I decided to come here instead. It wasn't that difficult a decision to make really, even though I grew up an Evertonian. I felt I had more chance of improving as a player at Liverpool and I have never lived to regret that decision. It was the right choice for me to make and the fact I have played first team football this season proves I did the right thing.

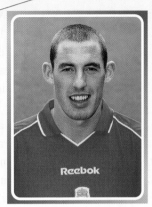

AND THE BLUES

DANNY MURPHY

It was always my dream to play for Liverpool. When I was at Crewe there was often speculation that Liverpool wanted to sign me and I must admit that was very exciting. Then when the move went through it was just a fabulous feeling. It's well documented now that I came close to leaving Liverpool because I wasn't doing myself justice, but I've worked hard over the last couple of seasons and am now enjoying my football more than at any other time in my life. It's a privilege to play for this club.

JAMIE CARRAGHER

I grew up supporting Everton – like a lot of the lads here did. You are either red or blue in this city and watching Everton was something which was drummed into me at an early age. I was a big fan as well. I still want them to do well and don't enjoy seeing that they have lost games, but I am totally committed to Liverpool now. I want to win derbies as much as anybody, for example, even though we play against the side I supported as a kid.

WWW.LIVER

WE MAY NOT BE ABLE TO BOAST ABOUT HAVING THE MOST FANS IN THE WORLD, BUT, DID YOU KNOW THAT LIVERPOOLFC.TV IS OFFICIALLY THE BIGGEST FOOTBALL WEBSITE IN THE WORLD? YES REALLY! BIGGER THAN REAL MADRID, ROMA, BAYERN MUNICH, MANCHESTER UNITED ETC ETC.

Since its launch in April 2001, Liverpoolfc.tv has attempted to provide us with the most comprehensive news coverage from Anfield, as well as keeping the fans involved as much as possible.

Keeping us all updated through the website is hard work. The hours can be long and the website needs constant updating. BUT, don't feel too sorry for the boys and girls who sit at their computers bringing us all the latest news and comprehensive coverage from Anfield, because few jobs could be better suited to the dedicated Liverpool fan. Can you imagine having the chance to write about football every single day? The chance to interview players and management staff at Melwood? Having an inside track on all the comings and goings at Anfield? It must be sheer bliss.

And as if that wasn't enough, to keep the site absolutely bang up-to-date, some of the staff need to travel with the team to watch them play away in Europe!

Take the Galatasaray game for example. Two of the editorial team and the full-time commentator boarded a plane to Turkey. Before they left they had to check that phone lines had been installed in the stadium and that

POOLFC.TV

was some nervousness about the reception that might await them from the local fans, who have caused some trouble in the past. But their fears were unfounded. They were met by a young girl handing out flowers and the Turkish people couldn't have been more hospitable – although our intrepid travellers agree that driving through Istanbul in a speeding taxi is far more nerve-wracking than a penalty shoot-out in a Cup Final!

Once settled at the hotel, connections checked and a hasty meal eaten, it was off to the stadium to prepare for the big match and do a few pre-match interviews.

Finally, the moment everyone had been waiting for... Kick Off. The fans who had travelled out for the game were perfect and everyone had a brilliant time. The match wasn't the best and although the team put in a good performance, the draw was

disappointing, but the sight of 20,000 Turks jumping up and down at the same time more than made up for the lacklustre game.

As ever, once the game had finished and the post-match interviews had been conducted, it was down to some serious work for the website team as they laboured into the early hours to ensure that any of us who cared to log on would have the most up-to-date information in the country.

It's a dirty job, but somebody's got to do it! ●

their press accreditation had been confirmed – otherwise they would not have been allowed in to watch the match. The other absolutely essential thing to check is that they have internet connection from their hotel room.

So, back to the trip. The Liverpoolfc.tv team boarded the plane with the rest of the press pack. There

15 FACTS ABOUT...
MARKUS BABBEL

1 Markus was born in Munich on 8th September 1972.

2 Markus was a boyhood Liverpool fan.

3 He joined Liverpool on a free transfer from Bayern Munich in 2000.

4 His squad number at Anfield is 6.

5 He quit international football in 2000 to concentrate on his football with Liverpool.

6 Markus made his Liverpool debut against Bradford City at Anfield on the opening day of the 2000-2001 season.

7 In the treble season he played 60 games, scoring six goals.

8 Markus scored his first Liverpool goal against Stoke City in the record 8–0 win in the Worthington Cup.

9 Markus was in the Bayern team that lost in the final of the Champions League in 1999.

10 Markus played in all five of Liverpool's cup wins.

11 Markus was sidelined for the remainder of the 2001/02 season with Guillain-Barré syndrome, a serious nerve disorder.

12 Markus has 51 caps for Germany and has scored one goal.

13 He was in the Germany team that won Euro 96 playing against future Reds Patrik Berger and Vladimir Smicer.

14 In his final season with Bayern Munich, Markus helped the club to a league and cup double.

15 He made his international debut for Germany in 1995.

1 Vladimir was born in Decin, Czech Republic on 24th May 1973.

2 His squad number for Liverpool is 7.

3 He joined his great mate Patrik Berger at Anfield in the summer of 1999 when he arrived from French club Lens for £3.5 million.

4 Vladi's first game at Anfield was for the Czech Republic in Euro 96 when he came on as a substitute for Berger in the 2–1 win over Italy.

5 Five days later he scored his first goal at Anfield in the Czech's 3–3 draw with Russia.

15 FACTS ABOUT...

VLADIMIR SMICER

6 Vladi started his footballing career playing for local side Decin at the age of 11 before Slavia Prague came in to buy him at the age of 14 for a modest fee of £800.

7 He made his league debut for Slavia in 1992.

8 His second club was Sparta Prague where he won a Czech championship medal.

9 Vladi only made one appearance for the former Czechoslovakia national team back in 1993.

10 His favourite shirt number is 10 – after his footballing hero Diego Maradona.

11 Vladi scored on his first Liverpool appearance in a 4–1 pre-season friendly win over Feyenoord.

12 He made his league debut for Liverpool on 7th August 1999 in a 2–1 win over Sheffield Wednesday at Hillsborough.

13 Vladi's first goal for Liverpool came in a 3–2 win away at Watford in 2000.

14 Vladi also won a French league title with Lens in 1998.

15 In Liverpool's treble season 2000/01, Vladi made 49 appearances scoring seven goals.

15 FACTS ABOUT...

EMILE HESKEY

1 Emile was born in Leicester on 11th January 1978.

2 His middle name is Ivanhoe.

3 Emile was signed by Gérard Houllier from Leicester for a club record in the region of £11 million in April 1999.

4 He made his Liverpool debut against Sunderland and made an immediate impact when he won a penalty at the Kop end in the first minute.

5 He scored his first goal for Liverpool against Coventry City at Highfield Road in a 3–0 win.

6 His first goal for Liverpool at Anfield arrived on the opening day of the 2000/01 season with a fantastic effort against Bradford City.

7 Emile's first goal for Liverpool in front of the Kop arrived against his former club Leicester in the treble season of 2000–2001.

8 Emile started in all five of Liverpool's finals in the Worthington Cup, FA Cup, UEFA Cup, Charity Shield and Super Cup.

9 Emile hit his first ever top flight hat-trick for Liverpool in a 4–0 win at Derby County in October 2000.

10 Emile finished second top goalscorer at Anfield in the treble season with 22 goals, just two behind Michael Owen.

11 He made his international debut for England against Hungary in April 1999.

12, He wears squad number 8 for Liverpool.

13 His favourite shirt number is 10– Emile used to pretend to be his hero John Barnes during his schooldays.

14 When Emile signed for Liverpool he became the third most expensive English player of all time, equalled at the start of the 2001/02 season by Frank Lampard. Only Rio Ferdinand and Alan Shearer cost more.

15 Emile was a Liverpool fan as a youngster and when Liverpool won the European Cup in 1984 Heskey was just five years old.

1 Michael James Owen was born on 12th December 1979 in Chester.

2 One of Michael's proudest moment's was when he was named BBC Sports Personality of the Year in 1998. He was also runner-up in 2001.

3 Michael became the club's youngest ever goalscorer, aged 17 years and 143 days, when he scored on his Liverpool debut against Wimbledon at Selhurst Park on May 6th 1997.

4 Owen signed terms with Liverpool at the age of 11 despite Alex Ferguson trying to get him to sign for Manchester United.

5 At the age of 14 he created a new goalscoring record for the England under-15 team, a record which had previously been jointly held by QPR's Kevin Gallen and Reds colleague Nick Barmby.

6 Michael's first start for Liverpool was at Hillsborough against Sheffield Wednesday on the final day of the 1996-97 season.

7 His first goal in Europe for Liverpool was against Celtic in a UEFA Cup tie in Glasgow in front of over 48,000 supporters in 1997.

8 Michael's England debut was against Chile at Wembley in 1998.

9 His first hat-trick in senior football came against Grimsby Town at Anfield in a Coca Cola Cup tie in 1997.

10 His first Premiership hat-trick came at Hillsborough in an enthralling 3–3 draw with Sheffield Wednesday in 1998.

11 His first goal for England arrived in a World Cup warm-up against Morocco in 1998.

15 FACTS ABOUT...
MICHAEL OWEN

12 In his first full season Michael picked up the PFA Young Player of the Year Award.

13 Michael was an Everton fan as a boy.

14 The 2001 FA Cup Final will forever be know in folklore as the Owen Cup Final, as Michael's two late goals gave Liverpool a 2–1 victory over Arsenal

15 Michael's pre-match meal is boiled chicken, rice and potatoes.

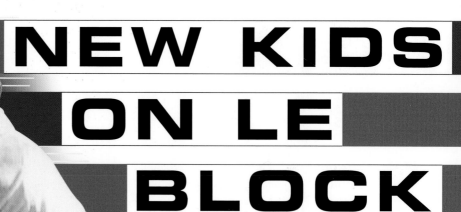

NEW KIDS ON LE BLOCK

GÉRARD HOULLIER IS CONTINUING TO SOW THE SEEDS FOR A GLORIOUS ANFIELD FUTURE BY SECURING THE SERVICES OF TWO OF THE HOTTEST PROSPECTS IN EUROPEAN FOOTBALL

French strikers Anthony Le Tallec and Florent-Sinama Pongolle will both be arriving at Anfield in 2003 after a deal was struck between Houllier and their French club Le Havre.

Both players have remained in France this year to continue their footballing education, but they will come to Merseyside before the start of next season with glowing reputations.

Manager Gérard Houllier said: "They are two gems for the future. I have watched them play many times and they will be good signings for us. It"s all about being clever in the transfer market these days. I arranged these deals before the European Youth Championships. After the tournament was over, everybody wanted them but it was too late. We has already done the deal."

Since the deal was struck, both

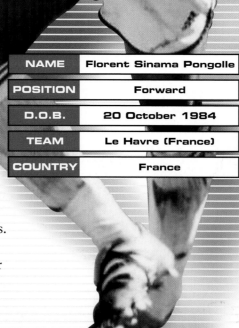

NAME	Florent Sinama Pongolle
POSITION	Forward
D.O.B.	20 October 1984
TEAM	Le Havre (France)
COUNTRY	France

youngsters have seen their reputations improve even further after helping France to success in the World Under-17 Championships last year.

Le Tallec scored three goals and won the Silver Ball as second best player in the competition while Sinama Pongolle netted nine goals and was named the best player in the tournament, having collected 36 of the votes from 44 available. He walked away with the Golden Shoe award for his goalscoring achievements.

Pongolle"s first goal in the final against Nigeria made him the highest goalscorer in the competition"s history, beating the record set by West Germany"s Marcel Witeczek in 1985.

Speaking after the final, Le Tallec said: "Being world champions, of course, is the greatest satisfaction. But then to also receive the Adidas Silver Ball, and to be chosen from among so many great players, is truly an honour."

Sinama Pongolle said: "This success is a collective one due only to our work together. Of course, neither Anthony

NAME	Anthony Le Tallec
POSITION	Forward
D.O.B.	3 October 1984
TEAM	Le Havre (France)
COUNTRY	France

nor I could dream of anything more extraordinary. I"d like to thank the rest of the team, because it"s due to our team mates that we could be in a position to win these awards. Being world champions represents a lot of emotions for us, but we have to keep our feet planted firmly on the ground because achieving success at the next level is something different altogether. We have to continue working and working, and then we will see what happens."

French coach Jean-Francois Jodar added: "They were decisive as strikers, but they also benefited from the rest of the group. You cannot have good results without exceptional players, and they were exceptional during this tournament. I am very glad for Anthony that he could help decide some games late in the tournament. I am really, really proud that Sinama Pongolle is the new record-holder for goals scored in this competition."

Both players are now thoroughly looking forward to their Anfield move and there's little doubt that, in years to come, they will have a major impact on the Premiership scene.

Pongolle said: "The fact that I am going to Liverpool to play with Anthony adds to the joy of playing there. We are confident because we know where we are going. I am not afraid at all of going abroad because actually France was abroad for me when I came here. It is a dream for us." Hopefully they will live their dreams many times in the red shirt of Liverpool FC. ●

ONES TO WATCH

THE LIVERPOOL YOUTH ACADEMY IS WORLD FAMOUS FOR PRODUCING SOME OF THE BEST TALENT IN FOOTBALL. SO DON'T BE SURPRISED IF THESE FIVE VERY TALENTED BOYS ARE TAKING THE GAME BY STORM VERY SOON.

John has recently started training with the first team at Melwood – a sure sign that he is on his way to challenging for a first team place at Anfield. A combative midfield player, he is a former captain of England schoolboys and has been with the Reds since the age of 10. He is a regular for the reserve team and starred in Liverpool's under-19 campaign last season.

Hughie McAuley's verdict: John is a great talent, there's no doubt about that. He works ever so hard in the midfield, he puts his foot in where it hurts to win possession but he is also very controlled and creative on the ball. He can create goals and score goals and he is one we are definitely looking at as somebody who can make the next step up. Training at Melwood will certainly help him.

NAME	John Welsh
POSITION	Midfield
D.O.B.	10 January 1984

David has broken into the under-19 team over recent months after impressing for Dave Shannon's under-17s. A regular at the heart of the defence, David is comfortable in possession as well as being a difficult obstacle for opposing strikers to pass. He has also represented England at youth team level.

Dave Shannon's verdict: David has had a very good 12 months. At this club we are always looking at players to move forward and progress and he has certainly done that. Individual development is a big thing for us and we watch all of the players very closely to see how they are performing. David has got better with each passing month and we hope that level of consistency can be maintained.

NAME	David Raven
POSITION	Defender
D.O.B.	10 March 1985

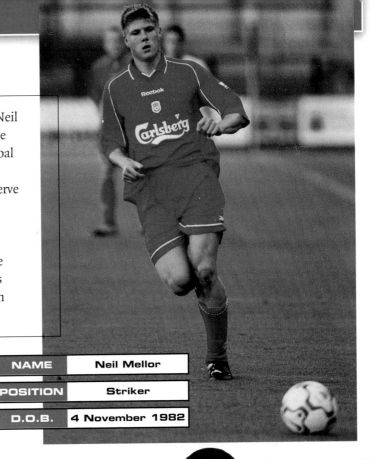

The son of former Manchester City player Ian Mellor, Neil is a big strong centre forward. He is exceptional in the air, works very hard and certainly knows where the goal is. His scoring record last season was nothing short of sensational as he bagged 45 goals in games for both the reserve team and under-19 teams. Definitely a star of the future.

Hughie McAuley's verdict: Neil has had an excellent season. He has a good eye for goal but at the same time his all-round game has improved a great deal. He gets into positions to score goals and even when they don't go in he never hides.

NAME	Neil Mellor
POSITION	Striker
D.O.B.	4 November 1982

NAME	Mark Peers
POSITION	Winger
D.O.B.	14 May 1984

Mark has been with the Reds since the age of 10 and is yet another example of a player progressing through the youth ranks of the club. He is blessed with exceptional speed and can play on either flank. He's not the tallest player in the world, but his nimble frame makes him even harder for the opposing players to deal with.

Hughie McAuley's verdict: Mark has good ability and has been given several man of the match performances over the past year. He's a very dedicated boy who works hard at his game. He has a great deal of natural talent, he's fast and he can get good balls into the area.

Mark is an England schoolboy international who has impressed for his country's under-17 team over the past year. He can play either in midfield or in attack, he possesses blistering pace and can contribute his fair share of goals during the course of a season.

NAME	Mark Smyth
POSITION	Midfield
D.O.B.	9 January 1985

Dave Shannon's verdict: Mark has been one of our most consistent performers at under-17 level. He is a young boy with a great deal of potential and the good thing about him is that he learns quickly. He takes advice and then puts it into practise on the field. We are only there to help the players and guide them – the rest is up to them. Mark has done himself proud of late and we will be looking for more of the same over the coming months.

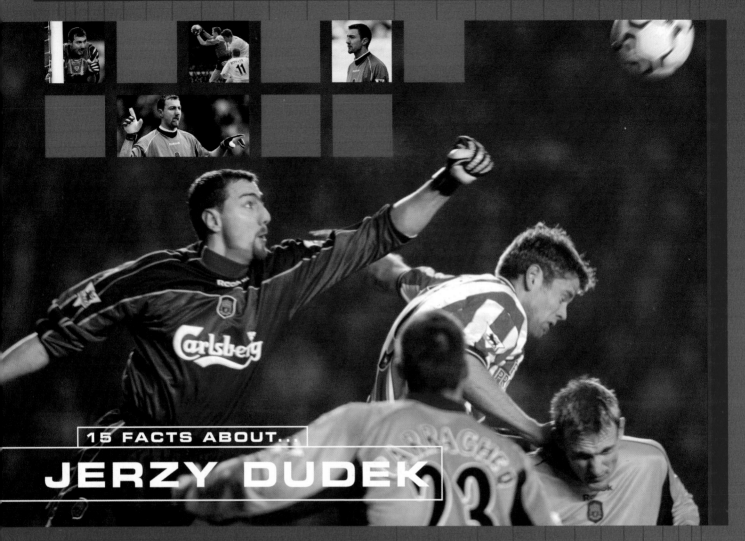

15 FACTS ABOUT...
JERZY DUDEK

1 The son of a Polish miner, Jerzy Dudek was born in Rybaik, Poland, on March 23 1973.

2 In 1995/96 he made his first team debut for Sokol Tychy but played only 15 games for them before joining Feyenoord.

3 Dudek was seen as a long-term successor to current Chelsea goalkeeper Ed De Goey.

4 He quickly became a cult hero in Rotterdam and during the 1998/99 season was voted the best keeper in the Dutch League

5 He made his international debut as a substitute for Poland in February 1998 against Israel in Tel Aviv.

6 Legendary Dutch coach Leo Beenhakker rates Dudek as 'the best goalkeeper I've seen in 30 years'.

7 His eye-catching performances for Feyenoord thrust him into the spotlight and many of Europe's big club's were rumoured to be tracking his progress.

8 During the summer of 2001, Dudek looked all set for a move to Arsenal but the £8.5 million deal fell through when the Gunners signed Richard Wright instead.

9 He admitted to feeling "devastated" after his move to the Gunners fell through – but he was more than pleased to accept Liverpool's offer.

10 He's regarded as a brave keeper with strong reflexes.

11 Dudek is the first Polish star ever to play for Liverpool – and only the second to play in the Premiership.

12 He made his Liverpool debut in the disappointing 3–1 home defeat against Aston Villa in September 2001. "It was not exactly the ideal start to my career," he said. However, Dudek was blameless for each of the goals.

13 Dudek played in this summer's World Cup finals after playing a starring role in steering his country to qualification.

14 Liverpool fans have already taken Dudek to their hearts, chanting "We've got a big Pole in our goal" at most Anfield matches.

15 Dudek is gradually mastering the English language, but admits he still has work to do before he is totally comfortable with the local tongue.

1 Danny Murphy was born in Chester on 18th March 1977.

2 Danny was signed by Roy Evans from Crewe Alexandra for £2 million in the summer of 1997.

3 In the treble season of 2000/01 Danny made 47 appearances, scoring 10 goals.

4 His first squad number was 24.

5 He now wears 13 for Liverpool.

6 His fantastic free-kick earned Liverpool a first victory at Old Trafford for 10 years against Manchester United in October 2000.

7 He also scored the winner at Old Trafford again for the second season running in Liverpool's 1–0 win in 2002.

8 Danny starred for England in the World Youth Championships alongside Michael Owen in 1997.

9 He struggled to make an early impact at Anfield and was loaned back to Crewe for the remainder of the 1998/99 season, but helped keep his former club in the First Division and avoid relegation.

10 Murphy made his England debut as an impressive second half substitute in the friendly with Sweden at Old Trafford on 10th November, 2001.

15 FACTS ABOUT...
DANNY MURPHY

11 Danny made his Liverpool debut as a substitute in a 1–1 draw with Wimbledon at Selhurst Park on 9th August 1997.

12 Danny scored his first Liverpool goal against Hull City in a Worthington Cup tie at Boothferry Park when he scored twice.

13 He missed the Worthington Cup Final through injury but played in both the FA Cup and UEFA Cup successes.

14 He almost left Liverpool in 1999 but after impressing in pre-season before the 1999/00 season Gérard Houllier kept faith with him and has been a key figure behind Murphy's revival at Anfield.

15 His second name is Benjamin.

1 Patrik was born in Prague, Czech Republic on 10th November, 1973.

2 Patrik joined Liverpool just after Euro 96 for £3.2 million from Borussia Dortmund.

3 Patrik's shirt number for Liverpool is 15.

4 Sparta Prague was Berger's first club at the age of 17, although he never signed a professional contract with them.

5 Patrik nearly left Liverpool in 1998 to join AS Roma after a bid from the Serie A giants.

6 Patrik was following in the footsteps of his uncle Jan Berger who played for Sparta Prague.

7 Patrik earned his first professional contract for Slavia Prague, but as he was too young his dad had to sign it for him!

8 In 1996 Patrik signed for Borussia Dortmund who won the championship during his first season at the club.

9 Patrik starred for the Czech Republic in Euro 96 and played at Anfield in the 2–1 win over Italy.

10 Berger scored a penalty in the Euro 96 Final but the Czech's lost on the golden goal rule to Germany.

11 Patrik has won the Czech player of the year award twice in 1996 and 1999.

12 He made his Liverpool debut as a substitute against Southampton at Anfield.

15 FACTS ABOUT...
PATRIK BERGER

13 In his second game he came off the bench to score twice in a 3–0 win at Leicester.

14 His first hat-trick for Liverpool came in a 4–2 win over Chelsea at Anfield.

15 Patrik announced his retirement from international football in March 2002 to concentrate on his club career with Liverpool

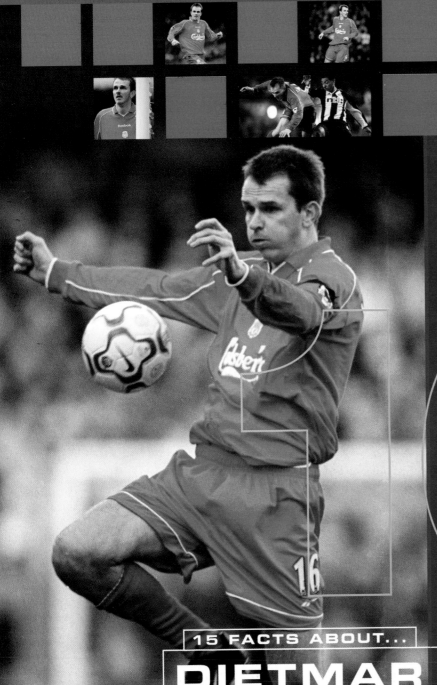

1 Dietmar Hamann was born in Waldasson, Germany on 27th August 1973.

2 He joined Liverpool for £8 million from Newcastle United in July 1999.

3 Didi made his Reds debut against Sheffield Wednesday at Hillsborough in August 1999.

4 His Liverpool debut lasted just 25 minutes against Wednesday when he limped off with damaged ankle ligaments.

5 Didi scored his first goal for Liverpool against Leeds United from a deflected free-kick at Anfield in a 3–1 win in February 2000.

6 Didi's all-time footballing hero is Johan Cruyff.

7 Didi went into the history books when he scored the last goal at Wembley Stadium from a free-kick for Germany against England in October 2000.

8 His all-time favourite film is *Raging Bull*.

9 He was signed for Newcastle by Liverpool legend Kenny Dalglish in the summer of 1998.

10 Didi's first club was Wacker Munich where he teamed up with his brother and his father who was coach.

11 A keen golfer, Hamann has a handicap of 20.

12 He joined Bayern Munich on his 16th birthday.

13 He used to support German side SV Hamburg in his childhood days and his favourite player was Kevin Keegan.

15 FACTS ABOUT...
DIETMAR HAMANN

14 Didi has an FA Cup winners medal with Liverpool and an FA Cup losers medal for Newcastle United.

15 Didi spent nine years at Bayern Munich under the guidance of Franz Beckenbauer, winning two German titles, a German Cup and the UEFA Cup.

NOVEMBER 4 2001, AT ANFIELD

LIVERPOOL 3 MANCHESTER UNITED 1

OWEN 31, RIISE 31, OWEN 51   BECKHAM 51

Referee: GRAHAM POLL

WHAT IS IT ABOUT LIVERPOOL V MANCHESTER UNITED THAT SETS THE PULSES RACING? MOSTLY IT'S THE PROSPECT OF WATCHING TWO TOP CLASS TEAMS WITH SOME OF THE BEST PLAYERS IN THE WORLD BUT ALSO LIVERPOOL FANS HAVE THE ADDED BONUS OF KNOWING THAT WE USUALLY WIN. TAKE LAST SEASON FOR EXAMPLE...

1 mins Liverpool start brightly and Smicer's run down the left flank unsettles the United defence.

5 mins The ball falls to Owen in a central position on the edge of the United box – but the Reds striker fails to connect cleanly and his shot goes wide.

9 mins Carragher clears off the line following good play by Van Nistelrooy. The Dutch striker flicked the ball over the head of two Liverpool defenders before Dudek forced him wide but he still managed to curl a shot towards goal that Carragher did well to clear.

14 mins Riise sets Smicer free down the left and his cross picks out Owen. Barthez is forced to make a diving save.

23 mins Carragher's cross from the right is fumbled by Barthez and in the resultant melee Murphy's shot is blocked by the legs of a United defender.

HALF TIME

49 mins Goal! Liverpool 2 – Manchester United 1. After Riise's attempted clearance, Beckham pulls a goal back for United with a left-footed shot that creeps inside Dudek's near post.

51 mins Goal! Liverpool 3 – Manchester United 1. United's joy is short-lived as Owen restores Liverpool's two-goal advantage, leaping highest to head home into an empty net after Barthez had failed to collect a cross. The visitors respond by bringing Solskjaer off and replacing him with Yorke.

FULL TIME

51mins

31mins Goal! Liverpool 1– Manchester United 0. Owen gives Liverpool the lead, latching onto a through ball from Smicer, he held his nerve to expertly curl the ball around Barthez and into the top right-hand corner of the net.

39mins Goal! Liverpool 2 – Manchester United 0. Liverpool win a free-kick to the right of the United box. Hamann taps the ball to Riise who drills an unstoppable free-kick past Barthez to double Liverpool's advantage.

— LIVERPOOL 2   MANCHESTER UNITED 0

60mins Liverpool break swiftly and a raking cross-field pass from Murphy picks out Smicer. The Czech charges past Brown but with a gaping goal at his mercy fires his shot into the Kop.

63mins Yorke shoots well over from outside the Liverpool box as United attempt to force their way back into the game.

66mins Dudek saves brilliantly, diving low to his left to deny Beckham.

80mins United are unable to break Liverpool down and the Reds defence copes comfortably with everything thrown at them.

— LIVERPOOL 3   MANCHESTER UNITED 1

THOMMO'S VERDICT...

Everyone will have their own opinions as to who was the best player, but I think Danny Murphy was the pick of the bunch. He got through so much work and did a great job for us.

In my mind he is the best midfield player we have at the club from a tactical point of view. He can play anywhere across the park and always do a great job. To say he is the best is some compliment.

I have to stress that Emile Heskey was astonishing for us as well. His contribution to the team is immense and I told him that after the game. He was up against two strong defenders and he held the ball up really well for us. He might not have scored but his worth to our side is huge!

LIVERPOOL Dudek, Carragher, Riise, Hyypia, Henchoz, Hamann, Murphy, Gerrard, Smicer, Owen, Heskey. **SUBS** Kirkland, Fowler, Berger, Redknapp, Wright.

MANCHESTER UNITED
Barthez, Neville G., Irwin, Silvestre, Brown, Butt, Veron, Beckham, Fortune, Van Nistelrooy, Solskjaer.
SUBS Carroll, Neville P., Scholes, Yorke, O'Shea.

JANUARY 22 2002, AT OLD TRAFFORD

MANCHESTER UNITED   **0**

LIVERPOOL   **1**

MURPHY 84

Referee: GRAHAM BARBER

1 mins Van Nistelrooy and Scholes get the game underway attaching the Stretford End. Gerrard's booked for a late tackle within the first minute. Beckham's free-kick deflected over the bar. Corner comes to nothing.

13 mins Heskey almost put through by Owen but the pass deflects off the No. 8's heel.

15 mins Giggs just fires wide of Dudek's post from inside the Liverpool area. A close shave for Thomms's team.

16 mins Murphy's free-kick inside the United half is easily cleared.

22 mins Blanc fouls Heskey 20 yards outside the United box. Gerrard's free-kick is deflected just wide. United break from the corner through Scholes and Giggs but Scholes fires wide. Danny Murphy sprints the length of the pitch to help out his defence.

HALF TIME

55 mins Barthez forced to race out of his area and clear with his head as Heskey chases a long Owen pass towards the United area.

59 mins Great passing spell by Liverpool in the United half only breaks down when Murphy fails to keep a misplaced Hamann pass in play.

60 mins Murphy blasts a shot wide and high from 35 yards out.

70 mins Brilliant Carragher block prevents van Nistelrooy getting in on goal. Beckham's shot flies just wide.

71 mins Owen knocks-down for Heskey just on the edge of the area but Emile blasts his shot well wide of the goal.

FULL TIME

84mins

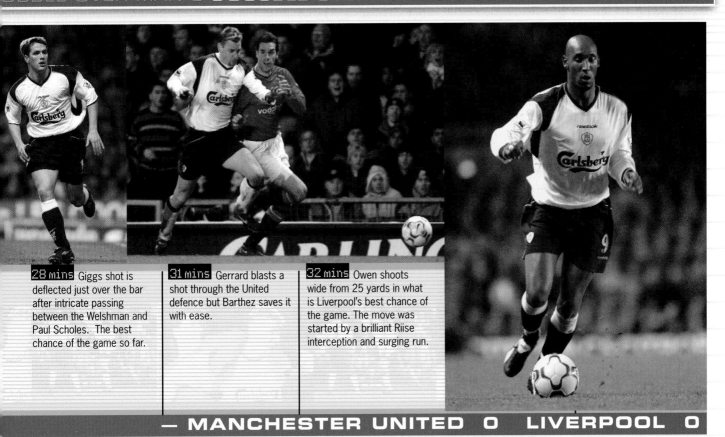

28 mins Giggs shot is deflected just over the bar after intricate passing between the Welshman and Paul Scholes. The best chance of the game so far.

31 mins Gerrard blasts a shot through the United defence but Barthez saves it with ease.

32 mins Owen shoots wide from 25 yards in what is Liverpool's best chance of the game. The move was started by a brilliant Riise interception and surging run.

— MANCHESTER UNITED 0 LIVERPOOL 0

73 mins A powerful Veron shot is punched away by Dudek.

77 mins An Anelka shot is just turned around the post in a goalmouth scramble.

81 mins Fantastic tackle by Gerrard on Phil Neville 10 yards from the Liverpool box.

84 mins GOAL! Manchester United 0 – Liverpool 1. Murphy ! After all the stick he got on Satruday, this was the best way to answer his critics! Anelka and Gerrard are both involved before Murphy loops his shot over Barthez.

— MANCHESTER UNITED 0 LIVERPOOL 1

THOMMO'S VERDICT...

I think it was written in the script for Danny to score tonight. There was never any temptation to leave him out after the stick he got at the weekend. That's because I believe in him and he repaid us tonight.

I am thrilled for the lad to score the winner again at Old Trafford. He worked ever so hard throughout the game and took his goal really well. He can run all day and is a great passer of the ball. He did well tonight and I'm sure he's on a

high after scoring the winner. He maybe just needs a touch more consistency in his game but he has done a great job this season. The criticism has happened to bigger and better players than Danny Murphy before!

LIVERPOOL Dudek, Carragher, Wright, Hyypia, Henchoz, Riise, Murphy, Hamann, Gerrard, Heskey, Owen **SUBS** Arphexad, Biscan, Anelka, McAllister, Berger.

MANCHESTER UNITED
Barthez, Neville P., Silvestre, Blanc, Neville G., Keane, Veron, Beckham, Scholes, Giggs, Van Nistelrooy.
SUBS Carroll, Butt, Wallwork, Solskjaer, O'Shea.

ON 29TH DECEMBER, 2001 MICHAEL OWEN, THE JEWEL IN LIVERPOOL'S CROWN, REACHED HIS 100TH LEAGUE GOAL AT THE AGE OF JUST 22! HOW MANY OF THESE DO YOU REMEMBER?

MICHAEL OWEN

KOP HERO, ENGLAND HERO,

Goal 11 v Leeds United 26th December 1997 3–1 (1)	**Goal 19, v Aston Villa** 28th February 1998 1–2 (pen)
Goal 12 v Newcastle United 7th January 1998 2–0 (1)	**Goal 20 v Bolton Wanderers** 7th March 1998 2–1 (1)
Goal 13 v Newcastle United 12th January 1998 1–0	**Goal 21 v Manchester United** 10th April 1998 1–1
Goals 14 and 15 v Southampton 7th February 1998 2–3 (2)	**Goal 22 v Coventry City** 19th April 1998 1–1
Goals 16, 17, 18 v Sheffield Wednesday 14th February 1998 3–3 (3)	**Goal 23 v West Ham United** 2nd May 1998 5–0 (1)
	Goal 24 v Arsenal 6th May 1998 4–0 (1)

Goal 1 v Wimbledon 6th May 1997 1–2	**Goal 5 v Tottenham Hotspur** November 8th 1997 4–0 (1)
Goal 2 v Wimbledon 9th August 1997 1–1 (pen)	**Goals 6, 7, 8, v Grimsby Town** 18th November 1997 3–0 (3)
Goal 3 v Blackburn Rovers 23rd August 1997 1–1	**Goal 9 v Crystal Palace** 13th December 1997 3–0 (1)
Goal 4 v Celtic 16th September 1997 2–2 (1)	**Goal 10 v Coventry City** 20th December 1997 1–0

Goal 25 v Southampton
16th August 1998   2–0 (1)

Goals 26, 27, 28
v Newcastle United
30th August 1998   4–1 (3)

Goal 29 v IFC Kosice
15th September 1998   3–0 (1)

Goals 30, 31, 32, 33
v Nottingham Forest
24th October 1998   5–1 (4)

Goal 34 v Tottenham Hotspur
10th November 1998   1–3

Goal 35 v Celta Vigo
24th November 1998   1–3

Goal 47 v Nottingham Forest
5th April 1999   2–2 (1)

Goals 48 and 49 v Leicester
City 18th September 1999
                                  2–2 (2, 1 pen)

Goal 50 v Southampton
13th October 1999   1–2

Goal 51 v Sunderland
20th November 1999   2–0 (1)

Goal 52 v Coventry City
18th December 1999   2–0 (1)

Goals 53 and 54
v Newcastle United
26th December 1999   2–2 (2)

Goal 69 v Arsenal
23rd December 2000   4–0 (1)

Goals 70 and 71 v Roma
15th February 2001   2–0 (2)

Goal 72 v Tranmere Rovers
11th March 2001   4–2 (1)

Goal 73 v Porto
15th March 2001   2–0 (1)

Goal 74 v Derby County
18th March 2001   1–1

Goal 75 v Bradford City
1st May, 2001   2–0 (1)

Goal 87 v Manchester United
FA Charity Shield
12th August 2001   2–1 (1)

Goals 88 and 89
v West Ham United
18th August 2001   2–1 (2)

Goal 90 v Bayern Munich
Super Cup Final
24th August 2001   3–2 (1)

Goal 91 v Boavista
11th September, 2001   1–1

Goal 92 v Everton
15th September 2001
                                  3–1 (1 pen)

Goal 93 v Charlton Athletic
27th October 2001   2–0 (1)

Goals 94 and 95
v Manchester United
4th November 2001   3–1 (2)

Goal 96 v Blackburn Rovers
17th November 2001   1–1

Goal 97 v Barcelona
20th November 2001   1–3

Goal 98 v Derby
1st December 2001   1–0

Goal 99 v Middlesbrough
8th December 2001   2–0

Goal 100 v West Ham
29th December 2001   1–1

LIVERPOOL BORN AND BRED

Goal 36 v Blackburn Rovers
29th November 1998   2–0 (1)

Goal 37 v
Sheffield Wednesday
19th December 1998   2–0 (1)

Goal 38 v Middlesbrough
26th December 1998   3–1 (1)

Goals 39, 40
v Newcastle United
28th December 1998   4–2 (2)

Goal 41 v Port Vale
3rd January 1999   3–0 (pen)

Goal 42 v Southampton
16th January 1999   7–1 (1)

Goal 43 v
Manchester United
24th January 1999   1–2

Goal 44 v Middlesbrough
6th February 1999   3–1 (1)

Goal 45 v West Ham United
20th February 1999   2–2 (1)

Goal 46 v Chelsea
27th February 1999   1–2

Goal 55 v Wimbledon
28th December 1999   3–1 (1)

Goal 56 v Derby County
18th March 2000,   2–0 (1)

Goals 57 and 58
v Coventry City
1st April 2000   3–0 (2)

Goal 59 v Tottenham Hotspur
9th April 2000   2–0 (1)

Goals 60 and 61
v Southampton
26th August 2000   3–3 (2)

Goals 62, 63 and 64
v Aston Villa
6th September 2000   3–1 (3)

Goal 65 v Manchester City
9th September 2000   3–2 (1)

Goal 66 v Sunderland
23rd September 2000   1–1

Goal 67 v Slovan Liberec
9th November 2000,   3–2 (1)

Goal 68 v Fulham
13th December 2000   3–1 (1)

Goals 76, 77 and 78
v Newcastle United
5th May 2001   3–0 (3)

Goals 79 and 80 v Chelsea
8th May 2001   2–2 (2)

Goals 81 and 82 v Arsenal
FA Cup Final
12th May 2001   2–1 (2)

Goal 83 v Charlton Athletic
19th May 2001   4–0 (1)

Goals 84, 85 and 86
v FC Haka
8th August 2001   5–0 (3)

MICHAEL OWEN IS ONE OF THE GREATEST GOALSCORERS
LIVERPOOL HAS EVER HAD – AND WE'VE CERTAINLY HAD A
FEW! WE ALL HAVE OUR OWN FAVOURITE MICHAEL OWEN
GOAL MEMORIES, BUT WHAT ABOUT MICHAEL HIMSELF?
CONSIDERING THE NUMBER OF GOALS HE'S SCORED,
YOU'D THINK HE'D HAVE FORGOTTEN ONE OR TWO, BUT HE
HASN'T AND HERE IS HIS RUN-DOWN ON HIS TOP 10 ALL
TIME FAVOURITE GOALS.

THE OWEN TOP TEN

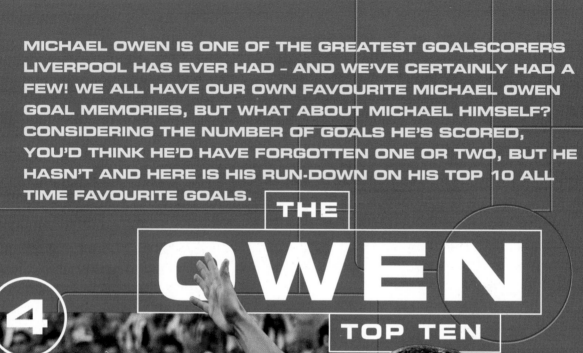

1	2	3	4	5
England Schoolboys v Scotland Schoolboys at St James' Park, April 28th 1995	**England v Argentina, World Cup Finals, St Etienne, France June 30th 1998**	**Germany v England, World Cup, Munich, September 1st 2001**	**Newcastle v Liverpool, St James' Park, August 30th 1998**	**Liverpool v Arsenal, FA Cup Final, Millenium Stadium Cardiff, May 12th 2001**
"I took the ball straight from the kick-off and beat several defenders before shooting past the keeper. I doubt I will ever score a better goal."	"It was the goal that changed my life. A pass from David Beckham set me running for goal and I finished it off. I never tire of watching it on video."	"My third goal in the 5-1 win had a bit of everything – a good first touch, a smooth run towards goal and a clinical finish."	"My hat-trick goal was one to remember. I was running at full pelt and managed to bend the ball past the keeper with the outside of my right foot."	"The second of my two goals won the cup for Liverpool. It will always have a special place in my collection. After accelerating past the final defender, I fired into the bottom corner – with my left foot. So much for it being my weaker side!"

6	**7**	**8**	**9**	**10**
Roma v Liverpool, UEFA Cup, Rome, February 15th 2001	Manchester United v Liverpool, Old Trafford, January 24th 1999	Liverpool v Nottingham Forest, Anfield, October 24th 1998	Liverpool v Grimsby Town, Anfield, November 18th 1997	Wimbledon v Liverpool, Selhurst Park, May 6th 1997
"I intercepted a pass, beat a defender and scored with a low shot."	"This was a rarity at the time – a headed goal! I scored after a few minutes when I climbed above everyone at the far post."	"I scored four. My pick of the bunch was a right-foot shot into the corner."	"The goal that completed my first hat-trick for Liverpool. I rifled the ball into the corner from outside the box."	"My debut goal in the Premiership. I had only been on the pitch as a sub for 15 minutes. My pace took me clear and I tucked my chance away."

1 Steven Gerrard was born in Liverpool on 30th May 1980.

2 He wears squad number 17 for Liverpool.

3 His first squad number was 28.

4 He was spotted by Liverpool at the age of nine playing for his local team. Frank Skelly from the Academy said: "He came in with a lot of boys and he stood out immediately."

5 Steven was 14 when he was taken on an Academy under-19 tour of Spain alongside a certain Michael Owen.

6 He made his Liverpool debut as a second half substitute for Vegard Heggem against Blackburn Rovers at Anfield on 29th November 1998.

7 Nine days later Gérard Houllier gave Gerrard his first start for Liverpool in a UEFA Cup tie against Celta Vigo at Anfield.

8 Gérard Houllier was so impressed at seeing Gerrard play in an under-19 game at the age of 17, that he immediately promoted him to the first team squad. Houllier said: "He was organising everyone on the park, so I certainly think he can become a captain."

9 Steven won the PFA Young Player of the Year award in 2001.

10 His first goal for Liverpool came against Sheffield Wednesday in December 1999 at Anfield.

15 FACTS ABOUT...
STEVEN GERRARD

11 Steven was handed his first appearance for England in 2000 by Kevin Keegan against Ukraine, and was called up into the Euro 2000 squad.

12 Steven's first goal for England came in the 5–1 drubbing of Germany in September 2001.

13 Steven's favourite shirt number as a youngster was 5 which was worn by his hero Ronnie Whelan.

14 In the treble season of 2000/01 Steven scored 10 goals in 50 appearances.

15 Steven's current contract extends until 2005, and he said: "I'm a Red, why would I want to go anywhere else?"

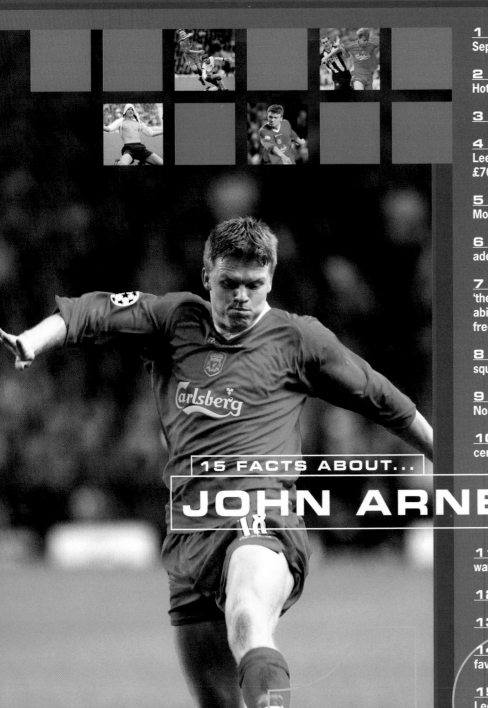

1 He was born in Molde, Norway on 24th September 1980.

2 As a boy he supported Tottenham Hotspur.

3 His first club was Aalesund FK.

4 In 1998 he came close to signing for Leeds but instead joined AS Monaco for £700,000.

5 During the 1999/2000 season he helped Monaco to the French title.

6 He is a left sided player who is equally adept in defence or midfield.

7 While in France he earned the nickname 'the Norwegian Carlos' – a reference to his ability to score spectacular long range free-kicks.

8 He was a member of Norway's Euro 2000 squad but did not appear in the first team.

9 Last year he made his full debut for the Norwegian national side.

10 He weighs 77kg and stands at 185 centimetres.

15 FACTS ABOUT...
JOHN ARNE RIISE

11 In his spare time he enjoys watching TV.

12 He drives a Ferrari.

13 His favourite film is *Titanic*.

14 Eddie Murphy and Sharon Stone are his favourite actors/actresses.

15 One of his closest friends in football is Leeds United's Eirik Bakke.

15 FACTS ABOUT...

NICK BARMBY

1 Nick Barmby was born in Hull on 11th February, 1974.

2 Nick fulfilled a childhood dream when he signed for boyhood heroes Liverpool from derby rivals Everton in July 2000 for a fee of £6 million.

3 In crossing the park, Nick became the first player to move from Everton to Liverpool since Dave Hickson in 1959.

4 His first goal for Liverpool in the Premiership came against, of all sides, Everton in the derby at Anfield, with a magnificent header right in front of the Everton supporters.

5 Nick's first club was Tottenham Hotspur whom he joined from the FA national school of excellence at Lilleshall.

6 He was 18-years-old when he was given his Spurs debut by Terry Venables and scored six goals in 22 Premiership appearances.

7 Nick had a two week trial at Anfield as a youngster, but Tottenham were the first to pounce and give him his break, right under the noses of Manchester United.

8 He was a member of the England under-18 team which won the 1993 European Championships, playing up front alongside Robbie Fowler.

9 After leaving Tottenham he joined Bryan Robson's Middlesbrough.

10 His England debut came against Uruguay on 29th March 1995.

11 His first goal for Liverpool came in a UEFA Cup tie against Rapid Bucharest in Romania.

12 In the treble season 2000-2001 Nick scored eight goals in 46 appearances.

13 During the UEFA Cup run Nick scored four goals – against Rapid Bucharest, Slovan Liberec and two against Olympiakos.

14 His squad number at Anfield is 20.

15 In the treble season 2000/01 Nick was one of two players to score in the Premiership, FA Cup, Worthington Cup, and UEFA Cup. Robbie Fowler was the other.

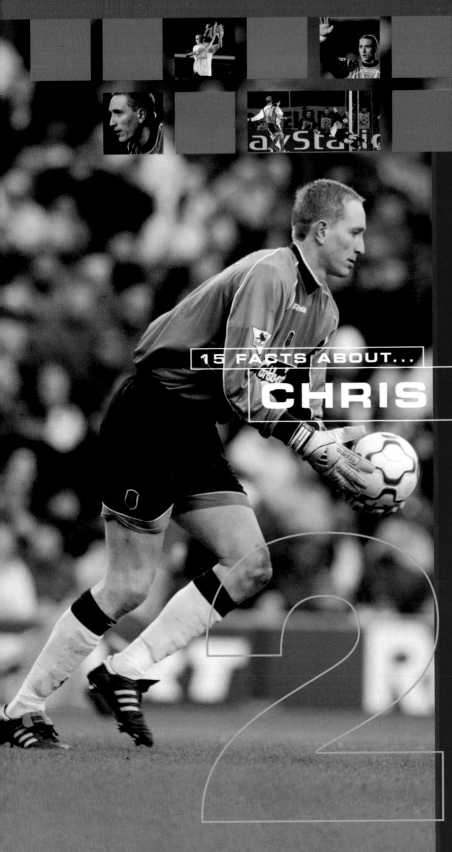

15 FACTS ABOUT...

CHRIS KIRKLAND

1 Chris Kirkland was born in Leicester on 2nd May 1981.

2 He joined Coventry as a trainee in 1987.

3 He is 6'6" and weighs in at 11st 7lb.

4 A former England youth international he made his under-21 debut last season.

5 Kirkland made his first team debut for the Sky Blues against Tranmere in a 3–1 Worthington Cup victory in September 1999.

6 He mad his Premiership debut on 14th October, 2000 in a 2–1 victory over Tottenham Hotspur.

7 Kirkland made 27 appearances for Coventry in 2000/01. He conceded 43 goals and kept six clean sheets.

8 Many other Premiership clubs were interested in Chris, including Manchester United, Tottenham, Everton and Chelsea.

9 Chris's only appearance at Anfield so far was for Coventry City in November 2000. He was beaten four times as Liverpool ran out 4–1 winners.

10 Before joining Liverpool in August 2001, Chris played just once for Coventry, in a 2–0 opening day victory against Stockport County at Edgeley Park.

11 Gérard Houllier never hid his admiration for Kirkland and it was an open secret that the Liverpool boss wanted to snap him up.

12 Kirkland has been a Liverpool fan all his life and regularly travelled with his dad on the bus from Hinckley to watch his heroes in action.

13 He made his Liverpool debut in the Worthington Cup defeat at the hands of Grimsby Town in October 2001.

14 Kirkland is the first goalkeeper in Liverpool history to play his first three games for the club in three different competitions – Worthington Cup, Champions League and the Premiership.

15 Kirkland was part of the England under-21s in the 2002 European Championships.

"QUOTE

"I had a vision when I came to Liverpool. In fact I had two visions. To make Liverpool the best side in the Premiership and to make Liverpool the best side in Europe."

GÉRARD HOULLIER

"Some people say I should give up football. Maybe I should give up breathing as well."

GÉRARD HOULLIER

"A former captain of ours said that myself and Phil Thompson would only drag the club down. He was right. We dragged them down to Cardiff three times in four months!"

GÉRARD HOULLIER

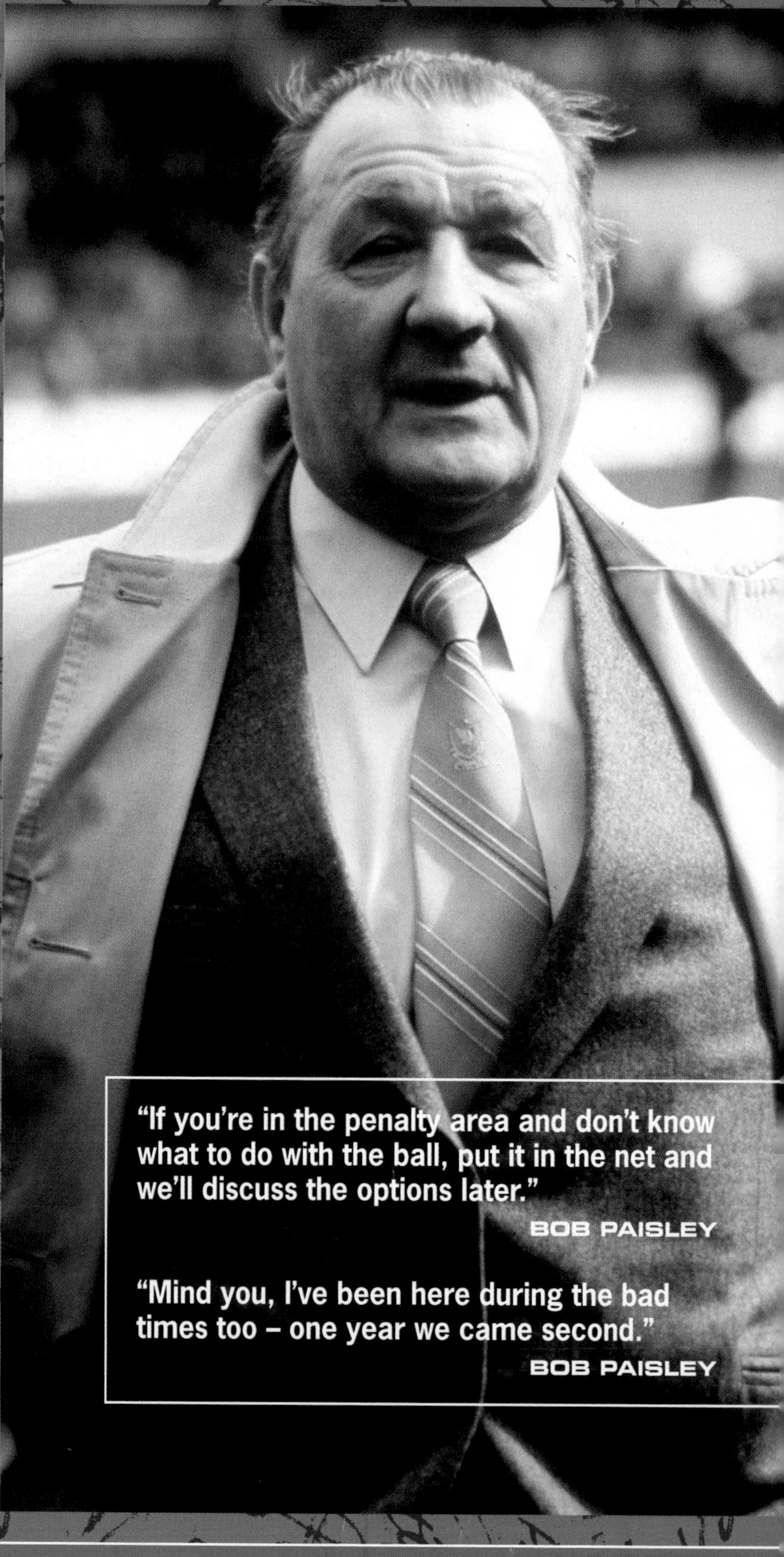

"If you're in the penalty area and don't know what to do with the ball, put it in the net and we'll discuss the options later."

BOB PAISLEY

"Mind you, I've been here during the bad times too – one year we came second."

BOB PAISLEY

UNQUOTE"

LIVERPUDLIANS HAVE BEEN ASSOCIATED WITH CLEVER, WITTY ONE-LINERS FOR LONGER THAN WE CAN REMEMBER. THIS TALENT SEEMS TO HAVE RUBBED OFF ON ANYONE ASSOCIATED WITH LIVERPOOL FC. HERE ARE SOME OF OUR FAVOURITES.

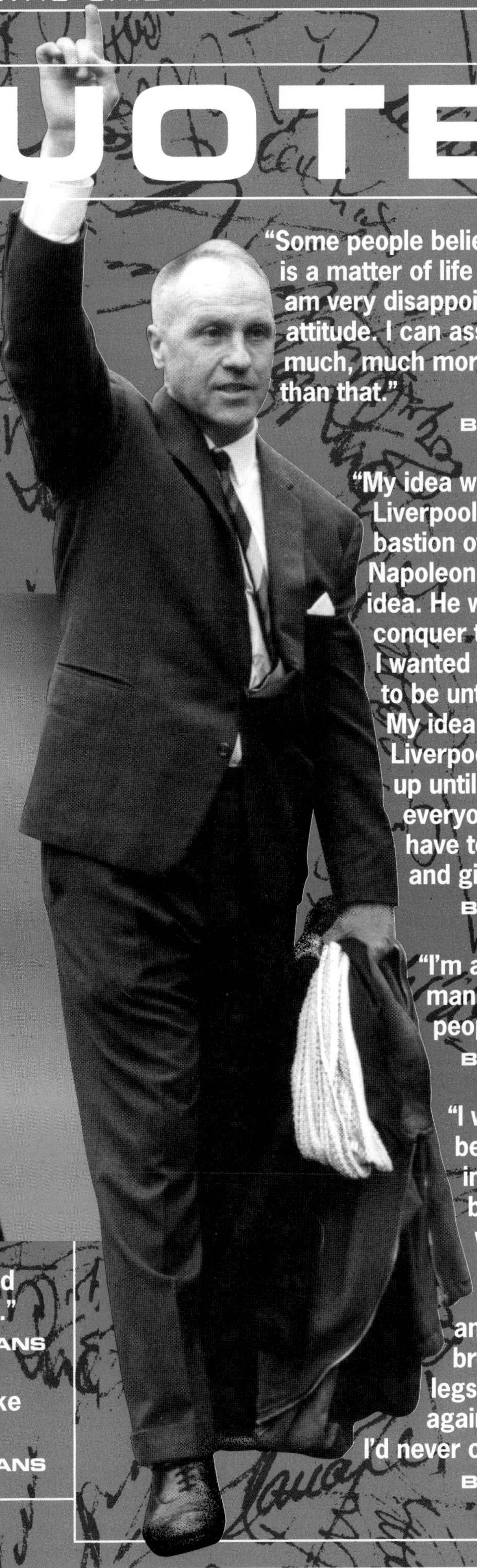

"Some people believe football is a matter of life and death, I am very disappointed with that attitude. I can assure you it is much, much more important than that."

BILL SHANKLY

"My idea was to build Liverpool into a bastion of invincibility. Napoleon had that idea. He wanted to conquer the world. I wanted Liverpool to be untouchable. My idea was to build Liverpool up and up until eventually everyone would have to submit and give in."

BILL SHANKLY

"I'm a people's man – only the people matter."

BILL SHANKLY

"I was the best manager in Britain because I was never devious or cheated anyone. I'd break my wife's legs if I played against her, but I'd never cheat her."

BILL SHANKLY

"I've been on this planet for 45 years, and have supported Liverpool for 42 of them."

ROY EVANS

"Liverpool without European football is like a banquet without wine."

ROY EVANS

1 Jamie was born in Bootle, Liverpool on 28th January 1978.

2 Whisper it quietly, but Jamie was an Everton fan as a boy!

3 Jamie came through the ranks at Anfield and played in the same youth team as good mate Michael Owen.

4 Jamie played in Liverpool's FA Youth Cup success in 1996 and showed his versatility by switching from midfield to centre half in the final against West Ham.

5 Jamie made his Liverpool debut as a substitute against Middlesbrough on 8th January 1997.

6 He scored on his full debut for Liverpool with a superb header against Aston Villa on 18th January 1997.

7 Jamie holds a record 27 caps for the England under-21 team.

8 Jamie has also captained the England under-21s.

9 He made his 200th appearance for Liverpool against Birmingham City in the FA Cup 3rd round tie at Anfield in January 2002.

10 Jamie was just four months old when Kenny Dalglish scored the winner in the 1978 European Cup Final against Bruges at Wembley.

11 He made his England debut against Hungary in April 1999.

12 His squad number for Liverpool is 23.

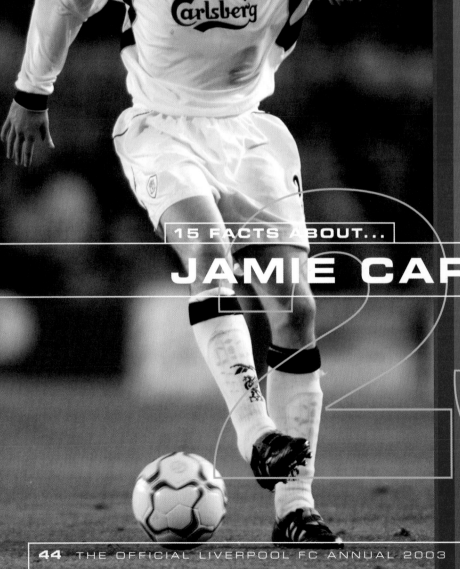

15 FACTS ABOUT...
JAMIE CARRAGHER

13 Gérard Houllier handed Jamie the captain's armband in a 3–2 win over Manchester City at Anfield in September 2000.

14 Jamie scored a crucial penalty for Liverpool in the shoot-out win over Birmingham City, in Liverpool's Worthington Cup Final victory.

15 Jamie is renowned for his versatility and has played in every position in the back four for Liverpool and also central midfield.

1 Igor Biscan was born in Zagreb, Croatia, on 4th May 1978.

2 His squad number is 25.

3 He is a Croatian international.

4 He was signed from Dinamo Zagreb for £5.5 million in December 2000.

5 Igor made his Liverpool debut almost immediately as a substitute against Ipswich at Anfield.

6 His first goal for Liverpool came against Crystal Palace in the Worthington Cup semi-final second leg at Anfield in January 2001.

7 Igor played right midfield in the Worthington Cup Final for Liverpool against Birmingham City at Cardiff's Millennium Stadium.

8 Igor turned down Ajax, Barcelona, Juventus and AC Milan to join Liverpool!

9 Besides Croatian, Igor speaks English and German.

10 Liverpool is one of the most popular clubs back in Igor's home country Croatia.

15 FACTS ABOUT...

IGOR BISCAN

11 Igor's footballing heroes are Marco Van Basten and Zvonimir Boban.

12 Igor's brother Hrvoje used to be a footballer and played in defence for Dinamo Zagreb, but he had to cut his career short due to injury.

13 Besides football, Igor has a love of basketball, which he used to play in Zagreb, and also likes tennis.

14 At 22 Igor was captain of Dinamo Zagreb.

15 When Igor joined Liverpool he had to get used to the idea of having no winter break, like they do in Croatia.

15 FACTS ABOUT...

GREGORY VIGNAL

1 Gregory Vignal was born in Montpellier, France on 19th July 1981.

2 He was signed by Gérard Houllier from Montpellier in October 2000.

3 His transfer fee was just £500,000.

4 He wears squad number 27 for Liverpool.

5 Vignal was at Montpellier for 10 years before joining Liverpool.

6 His only first team appearance for Montpellier was a 25 minute run-out in a friendly against Marseille.

7 Besides Liverpool, Vignal attracted interest from Barcelona, Celta Vigo, Valencia and Paris St Germain.

8 His idols are Michel Platini, Zinedine Zidane and Roberto Carlos.

9 He made his Liverpool debut as a substitute in the FA Cup third round win over Rotherham at Anfield in January 2001.

10 Vignal made his full Liverpool debut against West Ham at Anfield in February 2001.

11 Vignal was on the bench in both the FA Cup and UEFA Cup Finals.

12 It was Vignal who won the free-kick that led to Gary McAllister's dramatic injury time winner against Everton in April 2001.

13 He has been capped at youth and junior level with France.

14 He is a France under-21 international.

15 He won an Under-18 European Championship medal with France in 1999/00.

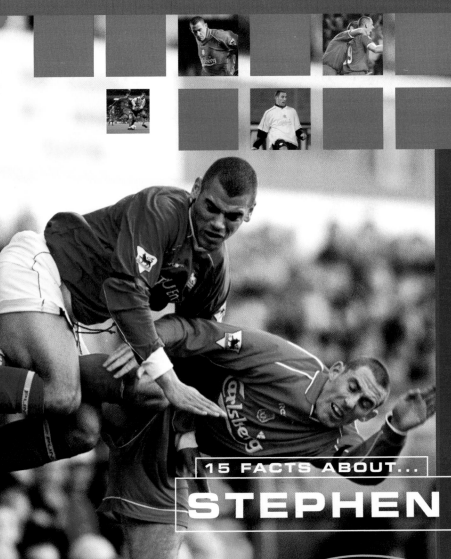

1 Stephen Wright was born in Liverpool on 8th February 1980.

2 He is captain of the Liverpool Reserve team.

3 He wears squad number 29 for Liverpool.

4 His dad John is on the Liverpool coaching staff.

5 Stephen is a regular in the England under-21 team.

6 Stephen had a loan spell at Crewe for the whole of the 1999/00 season.

7 He made his Liverpool debut as a half-time substitute for Markus Babbel during the record 8–0 Worthington Cup win at Stoke City in November 2000.

8 Wright made his Premiership debut as a substitute for the injured Markus Babbel in the 3-0 win over West Ham at Anfield in February 2000, and made a good impression too, helping set up the second goal for Robbie Fowler.

9 His first start for Liverpool came against Tranmere Rovers in an FA Cup quarter-final clash at Prenton Park on 11th March 2001.

15 FACTS ABOUT...
STEPHEN WRIGHT

10 Wright used to support Everton!

11 His first goal for Liverpool arrived in front of the Kop in a crucial 2–0 Champions League win over Borussia Dortmund at Anfield, on 30thOctober 2001.

12 His best mate at Anfield is Steven Gerrard.

13 He was sent-off for England under-21s against Germany in a case of mistaken identity. A Manchester United player committed the foul but the French referee thought it was Wright and showed the Reds star the red card!

14 Wright played in the same Liverpool youth team as Michael Owen and Steven Gerrard.

15 His boyhood hero was former team-mate Robbie Fowler.

TEST YOUR KNOWLEDGE

JUST HOW MUCH OF A KOPITE ARE YOU? USE YOUR KNOWLEDGE OF YOUR FAVOURITE TEAM TO ANSWER THE QUESTIONS BELOW, WHILE THE SPOT THE BALL PICTURES WILL TEST YOUR FOOTBALL PROWESS

FOR ALL THE ANSWERS TURN TO PAGE 62

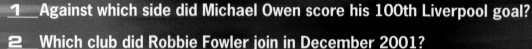

1 Against which side did Michael Owen score his 100th Liverpool goal?

2 Which club did Robbie Fowler join in December 2001?

3 Name the player Liverpool signed on loan from Paris St Germain in January 2002.

4 Liverpool have beaten Manchester United twice in a row at Old Trafford. Who scored the winning goal on both occasions?

5 Which club did Sander Westerveld sign for during the last close-season?

6 Name the two goalkeepers brought in to replace the departing Dutchman.

7 Name three Liverpool born players in the current squad

8 What is the name of Liverpool's physiotherapist?

9 Which club did Liverpool by El Hadji Diouf from??

10 Who is the most expensive player in the current squad?

11 Who wears the number 37 shirt at Anfield?

12 Name two players who have joined Liverpool from arch rivals Everton.

13 What nationality is goalkeeper Jerzy Dudek?

14 Whose free kick led to the winning goal in the 2001 UEFA Cup final?

15 Who scored Liverpool's first Premiership goal of the 2001-02 season?

16 Name the three sides in Liverpool's first Champions League group.

17 Who did Liverpool beat in the qualifying round of the Champions League?

18 Against which side did Nicolas Anelka score his first goal for Liverpool?

19 Which young midfielder did Liverpool sell to Tranmere Rovers in February 2002?

20 From which club did Liverpool sign Czech striker Milan Baros?

SPOT THE BALL

**USE YOUR SKILL AND JUDGEMENT
TO GUESS WHERE THE BALL IS**

SONGS FROM THE KOP

LIVERPOOL FANS ARE RENOWNED FOR THEIR TUNEFULNESS AND THEIR VOCAL SUPPORT. IN FACT, THE FIRST RECORDED SINGING AND CHANTING AT A FOOTBALL MATCH IN THIS COUNTRY CAME FROM THE LIVERPOOL FANS AND IT IS A RECORD WE UPHOLD PROUDLY. HERE ARE JUST A FEW OF THE CROWD FAVOURITES, SO NEXT TIME YOU'RE IN THE KOP, YOU'LL KNOW THE WORDS!

OH COME ALL YE - FAITHFUL

Oh come all ye faithful
Joyful and triumphant
Oh come ye Oh come ye
To Anfield
Come and behold them
They're the Kings of Europe

Oh come let us adore them
Oh come let us adore them
Oh come let us adore them

Li-i-verpool

FIELDS OF ANFIELD ROAD
(TO THE TUNE OF FIELDS OF ATHENRY)

Outside the Shankly Gates
I heard a Kopite calling:
Shankly they have taken you away
But you left a great eleven
Before you went to heaven
Now it's glory round the Fields of Anfield Road.
Chorus:
All round the Fields of Anfield Road
Where once we watched the King Kenny play (and he could play)
We had Heighway on the wing
We had dreams and songs to sing
Of the glory round the Fields of Anfield Road
Outside the Paisley Gates
I heard a Kopite calling

Paisley they have taken you away.
You led the great 11
Back in Rome in 77
And the redmen they are still playing the same way
All round the Fields of Anfield Road
Where once we watched the King Kenny play (and he could play)
We had Heighway on the wing
We had dreams and songs to sing
Of the glory round the Fields of Anfield Road

HOU LET THE REDS OUT
(TO THE TUNE OF WHO LET THE DOGS OUT)

Hou let the Reds out ? Hou - Hou - Houllier
Hou let the Reds out ? Hou - Hou - Houllier

POOR SCOUSER TOMMY

Let me tell you the story of a poor boy
Who was sent far away from his home
To fight for his king and his country
And also the old folks back home

So they put him in a Highland division
Sent him off to a far foreign land
Where the flies swarm around in their thousands
And there's nothing to see but the sands

In a battle that started next morning
Under an Arabian sun
I remember that poor Scouser Tommy
Who was shot by an old Nazi gun

As he lay on the battle field dying (dying dying)
With the blood gushing out of his head (of his head)
As he lay on the battle field dying (dying dying)
These were the last words he said...

Oh...I am a Liverpudlian
I come from the Spion Kop
I like to sing, I like to shout
I go there quite a lot (every week)
We support the team that's dressed in red
A team that we all know
A team that we call Liverpool
And to glory we will go

We've won the League,
We've won the Cup
We've been to Europe too
We played the Toffees for a laugh
And we left them feeling blue – Five Nil!

One two
One two three
One two three four
Five nil!

Rush scored one
Rush scored two
Rush scored three
And Rush scored four!

RED AND WHITE KOP
(TO THE TUNE OF YELLOW SUBMARINE)

On a Saturday afternoon
We support a team called Liverpool
And we sing until we drop (and we sail up to the top)
On the famous Spion Kop (of our red and white Spion Kop)
We all live in a red and white Kop
A red and white Kop
A red and white Kop
We all live in a red and white Kop
A red and white Kop
A red and white Kop

In a town where I was born
Lived a man who sailed the seas
And he told me of his pride
They were a famous football team
So we trailed to Anfield Road,
Singing songs of victory
And there we found the holy ground,
Of our hero Bill Shankly

STEVIE G
(TO THE TUNE OF LET IT BE)

When we find ourselves in times of trouble,
Stevie G runs past me,
Playing the game with wisdom, Stevie G,
And in my home, the Spion Kop,
We watch him jog, right in front of me,
Spreading balls with wisdom, Stevie G,
Let it be, let it be, let it be, Stevie G,
The local lad turned hero, Stevie G
And when the jubilant Kopite people,
All living in The Park agree,
That we all know the answer, Stevie G,
And although we may all be fooled,
There is still a chance that we will see,
The footballing phenomenon, Stevie G,
Let it be, let it be, let it be, Stevie G,
Spreading balls with wisdom, Stevie G
And when the night is cloudy,
There is still a man that we all see,
A young, committed Kopite, Stevie G,
Playing to the sound of music,
Stevie G runs past me,
Playing the game with wisdom, Stevie G,
Let it be, let it be, let it be, Stevie G
For we all know the answer, his name is Stevie G

Anh heres the mighty Toshack to do it once again.

We Love you Liverpool we do. We Love you Liverpool we do.
We Love you Liverpool we do. Oh Liverpool we love you.

We've won the league, we've won the cup,
We're masters of the game.
And just to prove how good we are
We'll do it all again.

We've got another team to beat and so we've got to try
'Cos we're the best in all the land
And that's the reason why.

We Love you Liverpool we do. We Love you Liverpool we do.
We Love you Liverpool we do. Oh Liverpool we love you.

WE LOVE YOU LIVERPOOL

We Love you Liverpool we do. We Love you Liverpool we do.
We Love you Liverpool we do. Oh Liverpool we love you.

Shankly is our hero, he showed us how to play
The mighty reds of Europe are out to win today
He made a team of champions, with every man a king
And every game we love to win and this is what we sing.

We Love you Liverpool we do. We Love you Liverpool we do.
We Love you Liverpool we do. Oh Liverpool we love you.

Clemence is our goalie, the best there is around
And Keegan is the greatest that Shankly ever found
Heighway is our favourite, a wizard of the game

15 FACTS ABOUT...

JARI LITMANEN

1 Jari was born in Lahti, Finland on 20th February 1971.

2 Jari fulfilled a dream when he signed for his childhood heroes Liverpool on a free transfer from Barcelona in February 2001.

3 Jari equalled the Finland international scoring record in March 2002 when his two goals against Portugal took him level with Ari Hjelm on 21.

4 His first goal for Liverpool arrived at the Stadium of Light when he equalised from the penalty spot in a 1–1 draw with Sunderland.

5 Jari has won eight Finnish player of the year awards in the last 10 years. Anfield and international team-mate Sami Hyypia won the other two.

6 Jari became the third Finn to sign for Liverpool after Sami Hyypia and young striker Daniel Sjolund.

7 When he arrived at Liverpool, his favourite shirt number was 7. However Vladimir Smicer has that, Steven Gerrard has 17, Gregory Vignal has 27 so Jari chose 37.

8 His first goal for Liverpool at Anfield came from the penalty spot in a 4–2 FA Cup victory over Manchester City in 2001.

9 At the age of 15, Jari chose football ahead of ice hockey and his first club was local side Reipas Lahti.

10 He won a Champions League winners medal with Ajax in 1995.

11 In 1995 Jari had his image adorned on a postage stamp in Finland as a tribute to his sporting achievements.

12 Jari made his Reds debut against Crystal Palace in the Worthington Cup semi-final at Selhurst Park in 2001.

13 Jari spent seven years at Ajax before he rejoined his former coach Luis Van Gaal at Barcelona.

14 Jari led Ajax to the Dutch league title in the 1993/94 season and finished top scorer with 34 goals, as well as picking up the Player of the Year Award.

15 Jari's first goal for Liverpool in front of the Kop was a screamer against Tottenham Hotspur in a 1–0 win on 22nd September 2001.

15 FACTS ABOUT...
BRUNO CHEYROU

1 Bruno Cheyrou was born in Suresnes, France, on 10th May 1978.

2 He is a creative goalscoring left midfielder but can also play as a striker.

3 Before signing for Liverpool, Bruno had been with Lille since 1997.

4 His brother Benoit is also with Lille.

5 He comes from a footballing family as his grandfather was president of Racing Club of Paris.

6 Bruno played in the Champions League for Lille this season and scored against Manchester United.

7 He turned down a move to French champions Lyon last season.

8 Bruno scored 11 league goals for Lille last season plus three in six games during the club's Champions League campaign.

9 He has yet to be capped by the French national team.

10 He won a French league Division Two championship medal with Lille in 2000.

11 Bruno Cheyrou officially signed for Liverpool on 1st July 2002.

12 Gérard Houllier, speaking about Cheyrou before completing the transfer, said: "He is a player we have been looking at for a while and I am sure he will fit into the Premiership without any problems."

13 He got married in Monaco in May 2001.

14 Liverpool had to splash out more than £4 million for his services.

15 He was also wanted by a number of top European clubs, including sides in Italy and Germany.

1 Jorgen Nielsen was born in Nykabing Falster, Denmark on 6th May 1971

2 He was recommended to Liverpool by former Anfield keeper Michael Stensgaard, who had to retire through injury

3 He spent the final three months of season 1997–98 on loan to Danish side Ikast and enjoyed a loan spell with Wolves during the following campaign.

4 He has made no secret of the fact that he would welcome a new career at another club, but a possible transfer to Wolves failed to materialise last season.

JORGEN NIELSEN

Joe Corrigan on Nielsen
"Jorgen hasn't played as many games as he would have liked but his effort and commitment in training on a daily basis has been top class. He knows it's difficult being a goalkeeper here and he hasn't really had a look-in over the years, but he has never let himself down when he has been playing in the reserve team."

LET'S NOT FORGET THE PLAYERS WHO ALSO PLAY AN IMPORTANT PART IN THE LIVERPOOL SQUAD. THEY MAY NOT GET TO PLAY IN THE FIRST TEAM AS MUCH AS THEY'D LIKE, BUT THEY ARE AN INTEGRAL PART OF LIVERPOOL FC.

1 Vegard was born in Trondheim, Norway on 13th July 1975.

2 He was the first signing of Roy Evans and Gérard Houllier in their roles as joint managers

3 The Norwegian international passed up the chance of Champions League football with Rosenborg to join Liverpool for £3.5 million,

4 Unfortunately his Liverpool career has been plagued by hamstring problems and he has been unable to put a consistent run of games together in the first team for two seasons.

VEGARD HEGGEM

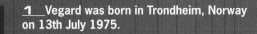

Gérard Houllier on Heggem:
"Vegard has had such a bad run of injuries and you can't help but feel for the boy. He has been out of action for a long time and we all hope he can come back again as soon as possible."

1 Bernard was born in Saint-Doulchard on 23rd January 1974.

2 Diomede is the only member of the Liverpool squad to have won a World Cup winners medal. The Frenchman played three times for France during their glorious triumph in 1998.

3 He made his Reds debut in the 1–0 UEFA Cup win over Rapid Bucharest in September 2000.

BERNARD DIOMEDE

4 He has been linked with a move back to France and has admitted he may have to leave Anfield to play regular first team football.

Gérard Houllier on Diomede:
"Bernard won the World Cup with France and so that tells you everything you need to know about his talents."

1 Djimi was born in Laval, France on 1st March 1980.

2 He spent last season back in his homeland after Liverpool agreed to loan him to French outfit Lens for the campaign.

3 Liverpool paid Laval £500,000 for his services in February 1999.

4 He made his senior bow at Hull City's Boothferry Park, and played in the return game at Anfield in the Worthington Cup games against Hull in September 1999

DJIMI TRAORE

Gérard Houllier on Traore:
"Djimi is a very talented boy and it was the right thing to do to let him spend a season with Lens. He will come back to us all the better for his experience and he will once again feature strongly in our squad."

A is for Anfield – the home of the Reds and one of the most famous stadiums in world football.

B is for Barclay – the club's first manager way back in 1892.

C is for Cardiff – the city where Gérard Houllier won his first trophy as Liverpool manager – the Worthington Cup in 2001.

E is for Eighteen league titles – Liverpool's record total. Roll on number 19! Also for the Eternal flame which flickers outside Anfield in memory of the 96 who tragically lost their lives at Hillsborough.

F is for Four European Cups – No English club can come close to matching the Reds' achievements on the European stage

G is for Geli – the Alaves defender whose own goal handed Liverpool victory in the 2001 UEFA Cup final.

H is for Hillsborough – The 96 will never be forgotten. Also for Houllier – the man who will take us back to the top of the English game.

I is for Istanbul – where Liverpool played for the first time last season against Galatasaray in the Champions League.

J is for Jones – Rob was one of English football's most outstanding talents before a knee injury cut short his promising career.

THE DEFINITIVE

A-Z

OF LIVERPOOL

D is for Dalglish – arguably the club's greatest ever player. Also for Dortmund – who will never forget the UEFA Cup final v Alaves in the German city.

K is for Kop – the most famous stand in world football! Enough said.

L is for Liver Bird – the club's emblem. Also for Liverpoolfc.tv – the club's official website and the most visited football website in the world.

M is for managers – and Liverpool have had some of the best down the years. Shankly, Paisley, Fagan and Dalglish to name a few. Who would bet against Houllier going down as an Anfield legend as well?

N is for Neal – Phil Neal is the most decorated footballer in Liverpool's glorious history, with 14 winners medals to his name in all competitions.

O is for Owen – the European Player of the Year at the end of last season. Will he go on to become Liverpool's best-ever striker?

P is for Paisley – Bob led the Reds to three of their four European Cup triumphs – no other manager can boast that fact.

Q is for Queues – and the thousands of Liverpool fans who loyally wait in line every time tickets go on sale for a match featuring the Reds.

R is for Rome – the Italian city where the Reds silenced the home crowd in the 1984 European Cup final when Alan Kennedy's decisive penalty brought the biggest trophy in European football back to Anfield.

S is for Shankly – If Bill Shankly hadn't arrived at Anfield and turned Liverpool FC's fortunes around back in 1959, who knows where our beloved club would be today.

T is for 'This is Anfield' – the world famous sign which greets opponents when they enter the Anfield arena before games. It was erected by Shankly to frighten the opposition before a ball had been kicked.

U is for UEFA Cup – The 2001 final in Dortmund was arguably the greatest European final ever as Liverpool won 5-4 on the Golden Goal rule.

V is for victory – quite simply what Liverpool is all about. As Bill Shankly once said: 'First is first and second is nowhere'.

W is for Wembley – otherwise known as Anfield south during the glory days when Liverpool were bringing home trophy after trophy at the end of each success-filled season.

X is for Xavier – one of the latest recruits to Houllier's side, he followed in Nick Barmby's path and swapped Everton for Liverpool. Scored on his debut at Ipswich.

Y is for You'll Never Walk Alone – THE most famous football song in the world, adopted by the Kop as their anthem in the sixties and still sung as proudly today.

Z is for Ziege – the German international who enjoyed a brief spell at Anfield before moving on to join Spurs.

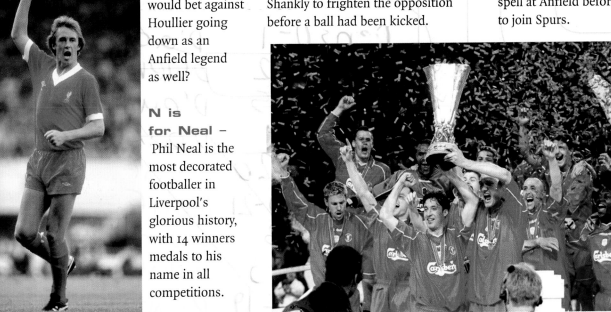

FIXTURES

PREMIERSHIP 2002/2003

DATE	OPPOSITION	RESULT	SCORERS	STAR MAN
17.08.2002	Aston Villa (a)	fulltim	4-6	owen
24.08.2002	Southampton (h)	Pens	10-0	Diouf
28.08.2002	Blackburn (a)	Pens	1-2	owen
31.08.2002	Newcastle (h)	Full	3-2	baros
11.09.2002	Birmingham (h)	Full	4-0	Diao
14.09.2002	Bolton (a)	full	4-2	owen
21.09.2002	West Brom (h)	Full	6-0	owen
28.09.2002	Manchester City (a)	Full	2-3	owen
5.10.2002	Chelsea (h)	Full	5-4	Diouf
19.10.2002	Leeds (a)	Full	2-5	Diouf
26.10.2002	Tottenham (h)	Full	7-2	Owen
2.11.2002	West Ham (h)	Full	5-1	baros
9.11.2002	Middlesbrough (a)	Full	1-3	owen
16.11.2002	Sunderland (h)	Pens	6-4	baros
23.11.2002	Fulham (a)	pens	2-3	Diouf
30.11.2002	Manchester Utd (h)	full	100-0	owen
7.12.2002	Charlton (a)	Pens	0-1	Diao
14.12.2002	Sunderland (a)	full	0-2	owen
21.12.2002	Everton (h)	Full	11-5	Diouf
26.12.2002	Blackburn (h)	pens	7-1	Diouf
28.12.2002	Arsenal (a)	full	14-20	Diouf
1.01.2002	Newcastle (a)	Pens	20-21	Diouf
11.01.2002	Aston Villa (h)	Pens	43	owen
18.01.2002	Southampton (a)	full	2-3	Diouf
29.01.2002	Arsenal (h)	pens	22-19	Diouf

FIXTURES ■ FIXTURES ■ FIXTURES ■ FIXTURES ■ FIXTURES ■ FIXTURES

DATE	OPPOSITION	RESULT	SCORERS	STAR MAN
1.02.2002	West Ham (a)		4-40	
8.02.2002	Middlesbrough (h)		60-9	
22.02.2002	Birmingham (a)		0-60	
1.03.2002	Bolton (h)		7o-0	
15.03.2002	Tottenham (a)		0-80	
22.03.2002	Leeds (h)		9o-1	
5.04.2002	Manchester Utd (a)		0-400	
12.04.2002	Fulham (h)		9oo-1	
19.04.2002	Everton (a)		0-4,000	
21.04.2002	Charlton (h)		5oo-1	
26.04.2002	West Brom (a)		0-500	
3.05.2002	Manchester City (h)		7oo-1	
11.05.2002	Chelsea (a)		0-40	

FA CUP DATES

Jan 4	–	FA Cup 3rd round
Jan 25	–	FA Cup 4th round
Feb 15	–	FA Cup 5th round
Mar 8	–	FA Cup quarter final
Apr 13	–	FA Cup semi-final
May 17	–	FA Cup final

BE ONE OF THE REDS

You follow Michael, Steven and Sami on match days, but if you become a Junior Supporter of the Official Liverpool Supporters Club you'll become a member of the Club and really get close to the heart of Liverpool FC.

You'll enjoy savings on official LFC gear and tours of Anfield. Plus, you'll certainly get close to the team because membership will get you free admission to reserve games.

Quite simply, The Official Liverpool Supporters Club is world class and if you want to be a world class junior supporter then you need to be a member. Just look below to see what you'll receive, then you can join today and support the Reds.

There are many benefits of joining the Official Liverpool Supporters Club. But one, that like the stuff your dreams are made of, is the chance to see Anfield like no other supporter can. When you are a member, you will be invited to attend the Liverpool FC Fans' Day at Anfield to watch the players train and sample the Anfield atmosphere. This opportunity is unique to the Official Liverpool Supporters Club - if you don't have the membership card, you don't get in.

WITH YOUR SUPPORT YOU RECEIVE ALL THESE BENEFITS

JUNIOR SUPPORTERS

ANNUAL £15 MEMBERSHIP

- Exclusive Video 'Goals from 1998-2002' - the Houllier years
- Exclusive Keyring
- An invite to attend the Liverpool FC Fans' Day
- A Personalised Membership Card
- Discount tours of the Museum and Stadium
- A chance to become a Mascot
- Membership Certificate from the Club
- Exclusive Results Wallchart/Poster
- 10% discount in The Club's Stores
- Free admission to Reserve Team Matches
- A chance to win a Signed Shirt
- A chance for your friends to join us
- A specially designed Liverpool Kit Bag

THE MOST IMPRESSIVE RED
THIS SEASON

Join the Official Liverpool Supporters Club and you'll receive your own membership card. This impressive Red will bring you 10% off merchandise in the Club's stores and by mail order, discounted admission to the Museum tour and free entry to home reserve games.

The membership card is valid for 12 months, so join now and use your card to save money on Liverpool team shirts and kit. Because junior membership only costs £15 you could save enough money with discounts over the season to cover the cost of membership.

CALL NOW TO JOIN
0151 264 2290
Please ask an adult to phone for you quoting 304 AD2

Or write to: The Official Liverpool Supporters Club, PO Box 205, Liverpool, L69 4PS

OR VISIT
www.liverpoolfc.tv
and click on Fansforum and Supporters Club to apply.

For details of adult or family membership call 08707 02 02 07

THE OFFICIAL LIVERPOOL SUPPORTERS C

ALL THE ANSWERS FROM PAGE 48 • ALL

1 West Ham United
2 Leeds United
3 Nicolas Anelka
4 Danny Murphy
5 Real Sociedad
6 Jerzy Dudek and Chris Kirkland
7 Jamie Carragher, Steven Gerrard, Stephen Wright
8 Dave Galley
9 Lens
10 Emile Heskey (£11 million)
11 Jari Litmanen
12 Nick Barmby and Abel Xavier
13 Polish
14 Gary McAllister
15 Michael Owen v West Ham
16 Boavista, Dynamo Kiev, Borussia Dortmund
17 FC Haka (Finland)
18 Birmingham City
19 Alan Navarro
20 Banik Ostrava